Stand Up,
Shake Hands,
Say
"How
Do
You
Do"

Also by
Marjabelle Young Stewart
and Ann Buchwald...

WHITE GLOVES AND
PARTY MANNERS

WHAT TO DO WHEN—
AND WHY?

Stand Up, Shake Hands, Say "How Do You Do"

New and revised edition

What boys need to know about today's manners

Marjabelle Young Stewart and Ann Buchwald

Foreword by Art Buchwald

Robert B. Luce, Inc.
540 Barnum Avenue
Bridgeport, CT 06608

STAND UP, SHAKE HANDS, SAY "HOW DO YOU DO"

LIBRARY OF CONGRESS CATALOG CARD NUMBER: 77-80159
ISBN: 0-88331-100-3

10 9 8 7 6 5 4
MANUFACTURED IN THE UNITED STATES OF AMERICA

To all boys, who

        through no fault of their own

    will eventually

       be men

               Ann Buchwald

To Clarence Bryant, William E.

    and Billy Stewart

               Marjabelle Young

Foreword

When I was a boy living in Hollis, Long Island, I didn't know anything about good manners. I was the terror of the neighborhood. Mothers wouldn't let me skip rope with their daughters, and fathers wouldn't let me eat dinner with their sons. I even got thrown out of a candy fountain once because I didn't know how to drink an ice cream soda (I blew out on the straw instead of sucking in). I wanted to do the right thing, but I just didn't know what the right thing was. Many a time when I was eating a peanut butter and jelly sandwich alone in the schoolyard, I thought to myself, "I wish somebody would write a book telling me what to do so I wouldn't be making so many social blunders."

Alas, in those days there was no one who realized the need for such a bible. The years passed and I kept searching for the secret of good manners. Every time I asked someone, I would always get the reply, "The secret of good manners is within yourself." Well, as you can imagine, this was no help at all, and I went from one school to another, one social group to another, always doing the wrong thing. It was a hard life. In the U.S. Marine Corps I was passed over for Pfc. because I didn't know how to hold a fork. In college they wouldn't let me into dances because I stepped on girls' toes. When I went to work, everyone else was promoted except me because I never knew the right way to address my boss.

I was a complete failure until I met my wife, who happens to be one of the authors of this book. She took pity on me after our marriage and taught me how to eat, how to converse with other people, how to show good sportsmanship, and how to wear the proper clothes. Once I learned the fundamentals of good manners, my whole life changed. I became the most popular person on the block. I had more invitations to parties than I knew what to do with. My boss finally promoted me; restaurants sought me out as a client; I was asked to lecture at universities. A whole new world opened for me, and my former schoolmates, who had shunned me as a child, now sought me out as a playmate.

I realized that if my wife could do this for me she could save countless boys from having the miserable existence I had, so I urged her to put down on paper with her friend Marjabelle Young, the etiquette expert, everything boys such as I was should know.

This she has done and you, my reader, are blessed. With this book you can avoid all the grave social blunders that I made in my youth because I didn't know any better.

So study this book and see if it doesn't change your life.

If, after three years, you don't see any difference in how people treat you, then I personally will give you your money back.

ART BUCHWALD
Husband of One of the Authors

Contents

Stand Up,
Shake Hands,
Say
"How
Do
You
Do"

Confidential Message

TO

_____   _____

(Name)   (Age)

There comes a time in every boy's life when he has to start behaving like a man. This behavior is called manners; if you have good manners you're doing the right thing, and if you have bad manners you're doing the wrong thing. Most manners are traditional—handed down from ancient times by kings and emperors, knights and warriors. They include such varied things as shaking hands when greeting someone, addressing superiors when asking a favor, and approaching a young lady on the matter of a dance.

There is nothing sissy about having good manners. West Point, Annapolis, and the Air Force Academy demand that all men who become officers learn the right way to behave in public. Wherever you go you will be judged on how you can handle a problem, whether it is dining out in a restaurant, attending a meeting, or dating a girl.

Most good manners should come naturally, and really depend on common sense. In this book we will set down a few guidelines that can help you get started and see that you have more fun as you enter the world of manhood.

We'll make it as simple and painless as possible.

1

Great Shakes

INTRODUCTIONS, GREETINGS, AND MEETING VISITORS

Every country and nationality has its own way for people to greet each other. Believe it or not, in some countries of Europe men kiss each other on the cheek. In others, they throw their arms around each other; and in the Far East they bow to each other before they start speaking.

In America we shake hands. When you grip another person's hand, you are telling him—or her—that you're happy to meet him, and a strong grip indicates a strong feeling of friendship.

1. You always stand up when you're introduced, whether to a man or a woman; and you remain standing until the other person has sat down. When a woman enters the room, you should also get up and remain standing until she sits down.

2. When introduced to a man or another boy, you extend your right hand and shake *his* right hand and say "Hello" or "How do you do?" Don't mumble, or the other person will think you're not really very happy to meet him. If the other person has just entered the room, you walk over to meet him, even if it means crossing the room.

3. When introduced to a lady, you wait until she extends her hand, and then you shake it.

(Many times, when meeting grown-ups and relatives, a boy will be asked stupid questions over and over again, such as "How old are you?", "Where do you go to school?", "How tall have you grown since the last time we saw you?"

These questions will probably drive you nuts, but grown-ups really don't know what to say to children, and you will have to put up with it.)

4. Always try to catch the other person's name when saying hello to him for the first time, and say your own name clearly. If you remember a person's name the next time you meet him, he will be in your debt for life.

5. When speaking to grown-ups or people you don't know, you should say "Sir." This is perfectly proper and shows respect. (You wouldn't call your Uncle Harry "Sir," though, unless he is very rich and you hope that someday he'll leave you all his money.)

6. On occasion, you will meet someone with a title, such as a doctor, or a major in the Army, or a judge, or a professor. You then give him the honor of addressing him by his title, since he has earned it. You address a priest as *Father,* a rabbi as *Rabbi,* and a Protestant minister as *Mister* or *Doctor,* if he is a doctor of theology. But when in doubt, use the word "Sir" and you'll never be wrong. (When your father brings his boss home, treat him with great respect—it may mean a raise for your dad.)

WHEN YOU ARE INTRODUCING SOMEBODY

Introducing one person to another person is one of the important things you will be doing for the rest of your life. You must say both names loud and clear. You might begin by saying, "May I present" or "This is. . . ."

There are three simple rules to follow:

1. You always say the woman's name before the man's, because a man is always presented *to* a woman (the weaker sex, you know).

"Gloria Jones, this is   (or "May I present . . . .)
George Smith"

2. You always say an older person's name before a younger person's name, because a young person is always presented *to* an older person:

"Mrs. Smith, this is   (or "May I present . . . .)
Martha Johnson"

3. And you always say an adult's name before a child's name, because a child is always presented *to* an adult:

"Dad, this is   (or "May I present . . . .)
Tony Brown"

Occasionally the situation will arrive when someone forgets your name. You can get him off the hook by saying your name while he's floundering.

This is a good thing to do because sometime you may forget *his* name, and then you hope he'll do the same for you.

HERE ARE SOME EXAMPLES OF EVERYDAY INTRODUCTIONS:

When you introduce your friends to your mother, say:

"Mother,   this is   Jane Powell
(or Johnny Powell)"

6

When you introduce a young friend to your father, say:

"Father, this is Mary Ellis
(or Jimmy Ellis)"

When you introduce a boy to your sister, say:

"Sis (or say her full
name if you prefer: My
sister, Connie Jones ...), this is   Bruce Gordon"

When you introduce your brothers or sisters to a friend, say:

    "Larry Smith,   this is   my sister Sue and my brother Tony"

When you introduce a small group of friends to one new-comer, say:

    "Mary Ellen Smith,   this is   Janet Jones, Helen Vance, Tommy Aherne, and Freddie Holmes"

When you introduce one new person to a large group of friends, say:

"Hey, gang (or "Quiet, everybody!)   this is   Jane Leslie (or Johnny Leslie)"

When you introduce your friends to your grandmother, say:

"Grandmother,   this is   Timmy McDermott and Tiger Brown, and his sister Nancy Brown"

Then look back at your grandmother and say her name, "My grandmother, Mrs. Williams"; otherwise they won't know if her last name is the same as your father's or if she is your mother's mother.

When you introduce your teachers to your parents, say:

"Mother,   this is   Miss Bedell"

or

"Mother and Dad,   this is   Mr. Johnson"

When you introduce one boy to a group of girls, say:

"Sue Wilson, Mary
Ryan, Judy Jones, and
Lisa Williams,   this is   Bruce McOliver"

When you introduce a group of boys to one boy, say:

"Willie Smith,   this is   Bill Anderson,
George Siegel, and
Eric Gordon"

Relatives and adults have a tendency to get your name mixed up with your brothers'. There's not much you can do about this except to say as kindly as possible, "I'm John, not Robert."

If you forget somebody's name, the best thing to do is say, "I'm sorry, I've forgotten your last name." But if the person happens to be a good friend and you forget his name, then you're in serious trouble. This is the only time when you may mumble.

It might be interesting to note that a handshake is also used in this country to pledge your word. When two men of good faith shake hands, it means they will keep their word, and this is more important than all the written contracts in the world.

Good Sportsmanship

An Englishman once said, "It isn't who wins or who loses that counts, but how you played the game." While this is tougher for Americans to accept, because we all want to be winners, the basis of sports is accepting defeat with style.

You are judged in life by the way you play the game, and for the rest of your life you will be winning and losing, not only at games, but in everything you do. If you're a poor sport in games, you'll be a poor sport in life. Those who are good sports in games are good sports in everything else they do.

Games are based on rules, and good manners in sports require nothing more of you than playing by the rules. The object of rules is to make it possible for each side to get a fair deal. When someone breaks the rules or complains about them, he is considered a poor sport; nobody wants to play with someone who cheats or who is always griping about the rules.

All sports are based on traditions; so are manners. This is the sportsman's code.

RULES OF GOOD SPORTSMANSHIP

Learn the rules and obey them, because the worst crime in sports is cheating. The way to avoid cheating is to play fair, to the best of your ability; and the test of a great sportsman is fighting hardest when he is losing.

12

Be a good loser by complimenting the winner on his skill after the game is over. Even more important, be a good winner by consoling the loser on his bad luck, not on his bad playing.

Support your partner or your team, and if you lose never put the blame on them. Never criticize another player; even pros make mistakes.

HERE IS AN EXAMPLE OF CHARLEY POOR-LOSER AFTER A GAME:

"It wasn't my fault. No one ever threw the ball to me. The quarterback never let me run a play; when I did get the ball, no one blocked for me and the other side was cheating, etc., etc., etc. . . ."

NOW HERE IS CHARLEY GOOD-LOSER SPEAKING:

"We had tough luck. Our team played its heart out, but the other side outplayed us. Maybe if we'd had a few breaks . . . but what the heck, we'll beat them next time."

LISTEN TO HENRY POOR-WINNER:

"We really smeared you guys. I thought you were going to give us a fight, but it wasn't even close! You fellows ought to go back to practice."

HENRY GOOD-WINNER, ON THE OTHER HAND, WOULD SAY:

"Nice game, fellows! We thought you had us there, but we got some breaks. We'd love to play you again and give you another chance."

Good sportsmen never complain about: 1. The Rules, 2. The Coach, or 3. The Referee.

They don't make excuses about themselves or their team-mates. They don't do anything to distract people from playing the game.

They give their all to win or lose, and they accept the decision of those in charge of judging the game.

Locker Room Manners

Some fellows who can control themselves on the field in front of an audience lose their cool in the locker room. This is dangerous because you are judged by your team-mates and your coaches in the locker room, and if you get out of control there, they can't trust you on the field.

Don't use foul language in the locker room. It's out of character for good athletes, and it embarrasses other people.

Control your temper: Don't throw your helmet, towel, or a ball to the ground; don't shake your fist or holler in anger at anyone. No one respects a person who can't keep his temper under ice.

Don't spit in locker rooms or showers.

Don't leave hot showers running, don't throw tissue on the floor, and always, always flush the toilet after using it.

Don't snap towels. It may be great fun, but can lead to serious injury, especially to the eyes.

Keep gear clean and in playing condition. Air your gear properly to allow for drying and to minimize formation of mold, fungi and odors.

Spectator Sports

As you grow older you will become more and more a spectator at sporting events. At some, such as football, base-ball, horse racing, hockey, and track meets, you can shout to your heart's content. But at others, like golf and tennis, you must remain quiet until the player has made his shot, or—in the case of tennis—until the player has made his point.

Razzing players on a football or baseball field may be good fun, but it isn't good sportsmanship. You have to assume that the people on the field are doing their best, and nobody likes to be razzed or booed. Before doing either one, try to put yourself in the player's place; see how you would feel if the fans were booing you.

As you grow older, you may go to the horse races, and if you are as lucky as most people at a race track, your horse will lose. Don't boo a horse if he does. He has feelings, too.

Mail Call

Everyone reading this book will spend a large portion of his life writing letters. There are all sorts of letters that men should know how to write, such as business letters, letters to friends, letters to relatives, thank-you notes, and even love letters.

We can't tell you how to write love letters, but we can help you with other kinds of mail.

At your age, the letter you will most frequently have to write is a thank-you note, thanking someone for a gift. Aunt Doris, or Grandmother Jones, or Cousin Charley get a big thrill out of hearing from you when they send you a present, and we have discovered that those who send thank-you notes are more likely to get future presents than those who don't. (But that isn't the reason we send them—or is it?)

In any case, when you thank someone for a gift, be sure that you mention what the gift was, and say something about it so the person who sent it knows it pleased you. Thank-you notes should be sent no later than one week after you receive a gift.

HERE ARE SOME SAMPLES OF THANK-YOU NOTES:

Letter—With the date and address in the lower left-hand corner under your signature:

> Dear Grandmother,
>
> Thank you for the book ends. I have always admired Abraham Lincoln, so it is nice to have Lincoln busts for my desk. Thank you for remembering my twelfth birthday.
>
> Love,
> Jimmie
>
> Sunday, October 28, 19—
> 522 South Tremont Street
> Kewanee, Illinois 61443

Envelope—With the return address in the upper left-hand corner.

> 522 South Tremont St.
> Kewanee, Illinois 61443
>
>
> Mrs. William Stewart
> 208 Jackson Boulevard
> Baltimore, Maryland 20003

Thank-you letter to a friend:

Dear Mrs. Varney,

Thank you so much for the gold cuff links. They are the first pair I have ever owned. Mother gave me a shirt for Christmas that needs cuff links; so now I'll be able to wear it.

I'm very happy that you and Dr. Varney will be here for my recital.

Best wishes,
Jimmy Brown

Sunday, October 28, 19—
522 South Tremont Street
Kewanee, Illinois 61443

Thank-you letter after you have visited a friend overnight or longer. This kind of letter should be written to your friend's mother and should be sent within three days after you get home:

Dear Mrs. Young,

Thank you so much for a great weekend in your home. It was wonderful meeting all your family, and you made me feel so welcome. It was certainly kind of Mr. Young to have the barbecue in my honor, so I could meet Jim's friends and neighbors.

My mother and dad send their best regards to you all. Thank you again.

Best wishes,

Jimmy Brown

Sunday, October 28, 19—
522 South Tremont Street
Kewanee, Illinois 61443

Business Letter—It's good to know how to type, because business letters are easier to read in print. Even if you can't type yet, here is the way a business letter should look:

```
                                    522 South Tremont Street
                                    Kewanee, Illinois   61443
                                    October 28, 19—


        Mr. John Jones
        Editor
        Washington Post
        1515 L Street N.W.
        Washington, D.C.

        Dear Mr. Jones:

        I am answering your ad for a paper boy.  I am twelve
        years old and am in the seventh grade at Horace Mann
        School.  I am interested in working for a newspaper
        because I would like to make journalism my career.

        I work on the school newspaper, and last year helped
        a friend deliver daily and Sunday papers for the Star.
        I certainly hope you will consider me for this job and
        will wait to hear from you by letter or phone.  Our
        phone number is 362-4556.

                                    Sincerely yours,

                                    James Brown

                                    James Brown
```

Thank-you note written on a folded "informal" card— You leave the front of the card blank and write on the inside, third and fourth pages of the card:

SOME THINGS TO KEEP IN MIND WHEN WRITING A LETTER:

If you're writing for a favor, be extra polite and write carefully so that the person can read your letter. For example, if you're writing to a television star for an autographed photo, tell him as briefly as possible how much you enjoy his show and how grateful you would be for an autograph. Be sure to put your address on the letter itself, since envelopes have a tendency to get separated from letters.

Always answer your mail. People who write letters to you deserve answers, and you will discover what fun it is to get mail regularly that way. Your grandmother and grandfather, and—if you're away from home—your mother and father, are always anxious to hear from you. Make your letters interesting. Tell them something you've done that they wouldn't know about otherwise. They're not interested in the weather or what time you got up in the morning. They want to know about *you.*

If you can write a good business letter, you can be a success in business.

If you can write a good love letter, you could become a famous novelist.

And if you can write a good letter asking for money, you can become a politician.

So practice, practice, practice:

1. Leave a wide margin at the top, bottom, and sides of your letters.

2. Address envelopes with the full names of the people you are writing to: Dr. and Mrs. William Stearn, etc.

3. Write out the street or avenue name in full; also the name of the state in full. Your return address can be on the back of the envelope or on its upper left-hand corner on the front.

4. If the letter is being sent air mail or special delivery,

print those words on the front of the envelope above the name and address.

5. Address a boy of thirteen years old or under as *Master* Sam Jones.

6. Address girls as *Miss* or *Ms.* Jacqueline Young.

7. Sign your letters and postcards with your full name.

8. When there are more than two pages to your letters, put the first page on top. Fold the letter in thirds, folding the bottom third up first, then the top third down over it. Insert the letter in the envelope with the salutation facing the back of the envelope; so the letter can be taken out and read without having to be turned around.

9. Write in ink, not pencil, because pencils are often too light.

10. A boy doesn't use *Mr.* until he is 14 years old.

Going Places

When you get right down to it, manners are really a question of style. A man with good style is admired, sought after, and asked back. A man with bad style is made fun of, shunned, and left with a sense of not being wanted.

At home or in small parties you are judged by close friends and family. When you go out, you are judged by strangers, and they can be even more harsh on you than people you know well.

Style tells the most when it comes to treating women—any woman——your mother, your grandmother, your aunt, or the girl you happen to be with at the time.

The greatest example of style is the famous story of Sir Walter Raleigh, who was walking with a lady when they came to a muddy street. Without hesitation, Sir Walter threw his cape to the ground in front of the lady so she wouldn't get her shoes dirty That kind of style gets you a page in the history books.

Most manners have practical reasons for their existence. For example, since Shakespeare's time men have walked on the outside of the sidewalk to protect ladies from the muddy splash of carriages in the street. Also, people used to throw their garbage out of windows; so it was much safer for women to walk as close to the buildings as possible; then they wouldn't get hit. To this day the man always walks on the outside.

GOING TO THE MOVIES

When you arrive at the theater, ask your girl if she wants to wait in the lobby while you get the tickets. If there's a long wait, she'll probably prefer to stand in line with you and talk. A boy removes his coat in the lobby and holds it on his lap after he is seated, or he checks it if there is a checkroom. Girls take off their coats after they are seated, by just dropping the collar and shoulder part over the back of the seat.

Wait at the head of the aisle until the usher comes. Ask the girl where she would like to sit, then tell the usher, "To the back, please" or "In the middle, please," etc. Let the girl follow the usher down the aisle. If there is no usher, you lead the way. When you spot some seats you'd like, say, "Will these do?" If the girl would like to sit farther down, she'll tell you. Stand with your back to the screen and let her go in first. Then turn around and enter, facing the screen, being careful not to bump people. Say "Excuse me" as you slip through. If you step on someone's foot, say "I'm sorry."

When others must pass in front of you, stand up and let the girl seated next to you turn her knees toward you in the space left by the raised seat. Tall boys should be careful not to shift around too much, since the person in back will have to shift, too. Don't tap your knee on the back of seats or stretch out so far that your feet reach down into the next aisle.

A word about concerts and live theater—Though everything may look the same as a movie theater, and the seating procedure is similar, beware of the laws of applause: At a concert, your first clapping will be when the orchestra leader comes out on the stage and bows formally to the audience. He then waits for complete silence before beginning the concert. Your next applause will be at the *very end* of each selection, so it's best to wait until you hear others clapping unless you're an expert.

At a play, you applaud at the end of each act or scene. It's not only rude but pretty disheartening to the cast when you sit there without even an attempt at clapping; after all, they're real people doing their best to amuse you.

GOING TO RESTAURANTS

Whether it's a pizza parlor, a drugstore counter, or the Ritz, there are certain manners to be followed in restaurants. When you go into a coffee shop or a fine restaurant, the first thing you do is check your coat and hat. If there is no checkroom, take them with you to the dining room and hang them on the rack near your table. A girl or woman never checks her coat, but you ask if she wants to check any packages she's carrying. A girl wears her coat to the table, sits down and takes it off after she is seated by just dropping the collar and shoulder part over the back of the chair.

When you go into a restaurant, hesitate at the door until the headwaiter or hostess approaches you. Tell him or her how many are in your party, then step back and let the girl follow the waiter to the table. Help her with her coat once you are seated.

A boy sits opposite a girl, or to the left of her. Women are always given the most comfortable seats.

When there is no headwaiter, you go ahead of a girl and find a table. Table seatings go this way: At open tables, women sit across from each other. At wall tables, sometimes called banquettes (pronounced *bonk-etz*), women sit in the wall seats. If a boy and girl are alone, the boy sits beside the girl at a booth or banquette table. A girl is always given the seat with the best view.

To order in a restaurant. The waiter gives a menu to each person. The girl then gives her order to the boy who passes it on to the waiter with his own order. First, study the type of menu: Table d'Hôte means one price for the entire dinner. A la Carte means you pay what each item on the menu is marked, so "à la carte" also means "expensive."

If the waiter asks a girl how she wants her steak (medium, rare, well done) or what she wants on her salad, she tells him herself. Dessert is usually ordered after the main part of the dinner is over, when the waiter again brings the menu.

You address a waiter as "Waiter," not "Boy." You don't clap your hands for a waiter or a waitress. When your patience runs out, you may raise your voice and say "Waiter" or, if it's a hostess, "Miss!" You do not yell, tap the table with a spoon, or lose your temper. Instead, stop another waiter and ask him to send yours to your table. Or raise your hand, not all the way like first graders answering questions, but high enough to be seen by a passing waiter.

If you drop your napkin or a piece of silver, signal the waiter to get you another. Don't pick it up yourself. If your food is not served the way you ordered it, or if you find some disagreeable object in it, simply ask the waiter to take it back. If you find silver or china that isn't clean, don't wipe it off with your napkin; ask the waiter for clean ones.

Later on, when you're the host, you'll ask for the bill by saying to the waiter, "Check, please." In fine restaurants the waiter will bring the bill on a tray. You study it to see that it's correct and to figure out the proper tip—roughly fifteen percent of the total. You put the tip on the tray when the waiter returns with your change.

In smaller restaurants, checks are paid at the cashier's desk and the bill is brought to you face down. You check it in order to know how much tip to leave on the table, since you'll be paying your bill on your way out of the restaurant.

When it's Dutch Treat, the girl gives her share to the boy to pay the bill. If there is any change for the girl, the boy gives it to her *after* they leave the restaurant, immediately after they're outside. Another way of 'going Dutch' is to ask for separate checks. Either way should be decided ahead of time.

When a woman stops to talk at your table in a restaurant, you stand up and remain standing until she has left, unless she is going to sit down and join you. If it's a crowded table, a half-rise will do, especially if the conversation will be just a brief one. Since a crouch is neither attractive nor good manners, you sit down if a girl finds it hard to tear herself away. You don't have to ask someone to sit down at your table when he merely stops to say hello. When a restaurant hostess comes to the table, you stay seated.

Strictly from a
Boy's Angle

Boys walk on the curb side of the street whether it's with one girl, two, or three. However, you don't do a ballet or a criss-cross at each corner. A smooth way of staying on the curb side when crossing a street and then turning a corner is to pause a second while the girl moves forward and away from the curb.

When you are walking down a crowded street, keep to the right side of the sidewalk. Don't try to buck the mainstream.

When two boys are walking with one girl, the girl walks in the middle.

If a girl stops to talk with a friend on the street, a boy always walks on slowly; the girl will call him back quickly if she knows the person well enough to make an introduction.

Boys always wait for a girl to say hello first when they meet on the street. If the girl doesn't say hello, a boy should just nod his head in recognition.

If a girl needs help crossing the street (when there's a lot of slushy snow or mud), a boy can help her by putting his hand lightly under her elbow, or by casually offering his arm (this means with the palm of his hand turned down,

30

not up as if he were carrying a tray!). When it's raining, a boy always holds the umbrella.

Boys let women go first whenever it's physically possible. Of course, if a girl opens a car door and hops out first, you don't ask her to get back in so you can show off your manners. And like all rules, there are a few exceptions:

• In church, unless there is an usher, the boy leads the way and finds a place to sit. Then he stands with his back to the altar and lets women enter the pew first.
• In a restaurant or theater where there is no waiter or usher to show you to your place, the boy goes first to find a table or a seat.
• In a crowd, a boy goes ahead of a girl to clear the way for her.
• When leaving a train, bus, or subway, a boy gets off first to help a girl out. He stands just outside the door to give her a hand if the doors start to close. (It used to be that men helped women out of elevators, but now with such crowds, men usually stand back until all women have left the elevator.)
• Getting in a taxi, a boy opens the door and says to the girl, "Let me get in first, so you won't have to slide over." Then, when she's in, he reaches over and pulls the door shut. This is particularly useful to know when you're with a girl in a long party dress.

Boys open doors for women—and the technique is this: You move ahead of a girl quickly to get near the door, pull it open, then step back. If the door is a revolving one, you step ahead of the girl, push the door to an open space, and hold it there for her to go through. In either case it's important to get yourself as much out of the way as possible to let her pass in front of you.

Always hold the door for people coming behind you; don't let it close in someone's face.

When you are with two or three women and they are in front of the door, the best thing to do is say, "Here, let me get the door for you."

Boys help women put on their coats, and with a bit of practice, it takes only a few seconds. You hold the girl's coat open a little below shoulder height (hers, not yours if you're tall, or she'll need a step ladder to get into it), then you keep it steady so she can aim first one arm then the other into the sleeves. Let's hope she does it gracefully. Once both arms are in, you can give it a final lift over her shoulders but she'll do the rest of the adjusting.

You help a girl take off her coat by stepping behind her at that crucial moment when the coat slides off her shoulders. Take it with both hands.

Boys take off their hats the moment they step into a house, a school, a church (except for a synagogue), a theater, a restaurant, an elevator, when the American flag goes by, when the National Anthem or the school song is being sung or played, and when standing on the street to talk to a girl or woman. You hold the hat, put it down, or check it, but you don't put it back on until you're actually leaving.

Parties

WHEN THE PARTY'S AT YOUR HOUSE
AND YOU'RE THE HOST

A party is one of the great indoor sports. Sooner or later, you'll be giving one—whether it's your own birthday party, a thank-goodness-school-is-out party, or just because it's your turn to give one. And though the whole reason for any party is to have fun, these are things you should know before you start:

FIRST, THE GUEST LIST

After your parents have given you permission to have a party, and have decided on the date, make up a list of friends you'd like to invite. Your parents will tell you how many people you may ask.

If it's a small party, don't brag about it at school, because some of your fellow students may be hurt when they aren't invited. Obviously you can't ask your entire class, but at the same time you don't want them to feel left out.

NEXT, THE INVITATIONS

No later than one week before the party, send out invitations giving (1) the date and time of the party, (2) the place, with your full name, address, and telephone number included, and (3) some description of the party if it's a special kind like a birthday party, a bowling or movie party, a Hallowe'en masquerade, or a Christmas party. If you don't

33

want to buy party invitations, make them yourself with construction paper and colored felt pens—your friends will appreciate them twice as much. Here are illustrations of the way written invitations should look:

YOU ARE INVITED TO
JOEL BROWN'S
9TH BIRTHDAY PARTY
ON SATURDAY, OCTOBER 10
FROM 4 TO 7 P.M.
ADDRESS: 4327 FIFTH AVENUE
TELEPHONE: 345-6789

I'm having a PARTY
on Saturday, October 10
from 3 to 7 p.m.
Hope you can come!
NAME: Joel Brown
ADDRESS: 4327 Fifth Avenue
TELEPHONE: 345-6789

* wear clothes for bowling

Invitations by telephone aren't quite as satisfactory as written ones, because they leave too much room for slip-ups on the correct address, or the right day and time. But if you don't have time to mail invitations, telephoning is the next best thing, providing your friends have pencils handy and will write everything down.

Now you wait for acceptances. If someone can't come, have a substitute name ready to invite, but *never* let the second person know he or she was invited only after someone else refused.

Tell your mother or father how many friends are expected; so that arrangements for games and refreshments can be made a few days before the party. You can be a big help on ideas for entertainment, whether it's a favorite game, a wild session of musical chairs, a home movie, or something special like a treasure hunt or a peanut hunt— where you hide peanuts in certain rooms of the house, then give a prize to the guest who finds the most.

If it's a party with girls, you must have a good record player, a few popular records, and a place to dance. If the party is just for boys, plan to play whatever games everybody likes best.

REFRESHMENTS

You don't have to have a lot of fancy foods at your age. Cokes, potato chips, pretzels, popcorn, and candy are sufficient for an informal party. If you're having a birthday party, your mother will usually arrange the refreshments, including the cake and ice cream. But you can help set the table, and decide where your guests should sit. It's a good idea to make place cards for a group of six or more; then there won't be a mad scramble for any one chair.

If it's going to be a buffet party, you can help arrange refreshments, plates, silver, and napkins on one main table;

then each guest serves himself and takes his plate wherever he wants to eat. (When the big moment comes, you will have to wait until your guests serve themselves before you fill your own plate.)

The party begins when the first guest arrives at the door. You should be clean, combed, and ready at least fifteen minutes before the hour, so you can answer the door. Until you're a teen-ager, your mother is really the hostess and will undoubtedly be with you at the door to greet your guests. You are the host, and your first duty—after you say hello—is to introduce any new friends to your mother as soon as they come in the house.

If you're having a birthday party your guests will—or will not—bring you gifts. Don't look to see if they're carrying packages in their hands. Sometimes a person will forget a present, or won't know it's your birthday, and you don't want to embarrass him by hinting that you invited him just for a gift.

On the other hand if the person does bring you a gift, take it from him and say "Thank you." Put it with other gifts and *open them all at once*. This is more fun for everybody. (Whatever the present is, exclaim with joy, even if you don't like it or you have another one exactly like it. You don't want to hurt your guest's feelings.) Never ask how much a gift cost, or even make a guess at its price.

You take each guest's hat and coat and hang them up, or you tell him where he can leave them. As each person arrives, you introduce him to anyone he might not know at the party. If it's a large group and he's a newcomer, you can say, "This is Sam Jones, everybody," but then don't walk away and leave him. Take him over to one or two of your friends and introduce him properly: "Sam, this is Jim Johnson and Fred Finch. . . ."

You shouldn't accept too many prizes at your own party. No one will take it to court if you win one or two, but in a series of games, it's better to give first prize to the runner-up when you, the host, win.

When refreshments are served, you wait until your guests are seated and served before you begin to eat.

AT THE END OF THE PARTY

You say goodbye to each guest at the door. If necessary you leave what you're doing and walk with him to the front door, where your mother will also say goodbye to him. You thank him again if he gave you a gift. Never yell "So long!" from another part of the house and leave him to find his way out alone.

Before you collapse, thank your parents for letting you have the party, and be a sport: help clean up the mess any good party makes.

WHEN YOU'RE INVITED TO A PARTY

When you receive a written invitation to a party, try to answer it right away. Say whether or not you can make it, but don't say, "I guess so," "I'll let you know," or "I don't care." When someone invites you to a party by telephone, it's good to say, "Thank you" when you accept, and "Thanks, anyway" when for some reason you can't go. In either case, you must first get permission from your parents to accept any invitation, and they'll want to know where and when the party is. Don't talk about it at school as some of your class may not have been invited.

If it's a birthday party, be sure to bring a gift. Help your mother shop for it, and don't buy something too cheap or too expensive. Your parents will probably have a good idea of how much to spend. Whatever the cost, don't mention it when you hand over the gift.

Find out what kind of clothes are to be worn. Informal parties might require a clean shirt but no necktie. More formal parties would demand coats and ties. If you're not sure, you can always wear a coat and tie, then take them off if the party doesn't call for them.

When you arrive at the door be ready to take off your hat as soon as you enter the house. Then say hello to your host's mother—or whatever grown-up is standing beside him at the door—and shake hands with her even before you say hello to your host. It's nice to thank your friend for inviting you; just saying it is a good ice-breaker while you're taking off your coat. Your host will tell you where to hang coats; always remember where you left yours.

As you join the rest of the party, shake hands with any boys or men you greet, even if they're close friends or neighbors.

When you are introduced to someone new, say "How do you do?" or "Hello" and don't forget the handshake. If a girl or woman enters the room, stand up and remain standing until she sits down.

Your host will decide when to play games and what to play. As a guest, go along with the plans even if they're not your favorite games or partners. A good party is like a good team—everybody has to contribute. Your host will also indicate when to eat. Never ask, "When do we eat?" It's a fact that party food is twice as delicious as meals at home, but take it easy with your first serving. It's better to have a second helping than to load up your plate the first time around.

When the party is indoors, don't horseplay around. Someone could get hurt, or you could break a lamp or some good furniture. If there's an accident and you're responsible, don't laugh it off. Help pick it up or clean it up, say you're sorry, then go on with the show, or you'll ruin the mood of the party.

A note: There may be one or two boys who will smoke at a party to look grown up. Don't become part of this nonsense. Smoking is no good for you, and instead of the other kids thinking you're grown-up, they'll probably think you're showing off.

When the party's over—and you'll know even if you don't have a watch, because others will be leaving—say goodbye to your host's mother and thank her for the party. Then say goodbye to your host or hostess, adding something like "I had a great time" or "Thanks a lot, the party was swell." Then leave. It's not polite to linger long at a party unless you've been asked to stay after the others go home.

Good Grooming

You probably won't buy your own clothes, and in many cases you won't have the last word on what you wear until you're a teen-ager, but these are the years when you can learn to make the most of the way you look and dress. For some reason—maybe because no one can read your mind—you will often be judged by the way you look, smell, walk, or stand, and by the clothes you wear. Until people know you well, they are liable to size up your personality and character by what they see at first glance. Everyone assumes the "Mud Pies" of this world have good clean hearts, but who wants to scrape away all that dirt to prove it? It's easier and smarter to learn a few facts about good grooming, then use them until they become good habits:

EVERY DAY

Try to look clean at the start and the end of each day, and at mealtimes. This means a shower once a day plus a good face-and-hands wash before breakfast if you take your shower at bedtime. Never come to the table or touch food without first watching your hands. Even if you "washed them before," do it again; they won't wear out. Always wash your hands before leaving the bathroom.

Brush your teeth properly at least twice a day. If you don't, your permanent teeth, due any minute now, will be sec-

41

ond-rate. Remember that food damage is done within fifteen minutes after eating. Use a mouthwash after each brushing.

Put on clean socks and underwear every day. Although some shirts, particularly colored ones, can go two days if you're careful, science has never found a way to make socks and underwear go two days in a row.

Make your bed before going to school each morning—Did you know that learning to make a bed properly is part of basic training in all the military services? Your mother will probably take care of changing the linen on your bed according to her schedule, but it's up to you to pull it together each morning.

Carry a handkerchief and USE it. Or grab a few clean tissues every morning in place of .a real handkerchief; man-sized Kleenex has now put the stamp of approval on tissues for the stronger sex.

Don't comb your hair in public. Both boys and girls question any boy combing his hair out there in front of everybody. Do it in your own room or the boys' room at school. Carry your comb in a hip pocket, not in your front vest pocket. People just don't like to look at combs! And never use another person's comb or brush, even in the family.

Keep your fingernails clean—the only way discovered so far: Use a nail brush every time you shower or bathe.

Use a deodorant especially if you're active in sports or ride your bicycle to school. It takes only two or three seconds after a shower or bath, and saves your friends or teacher the embarrassment of telling you about perspiration odor.

For your skin. Drink six glasses of water a day, and eat plenty of fruits and vegetables; they're insurance against a severe case of acne as you approach teen age. Since boys can't use cover-up creams that help girls through the pimply stage, it's a smart fellow who considers proper food (no fats, fried foods, extra rich desserts) the best medicine for his face.

Stand straight. It will make you look taller, feel better, and seem more grown up. Develop a manly walk and stride with enough muscular control to walk without clicking your heels or scuffling your feet.

Hang up your clothes at the end of the day. No one expects you to keep a model room, but when all the action's over, pick up and hang up your coat or jacket, your pants (they go on pants hangers), and deposit dirty clothes in the laundry hamper. Don't hang sweaters on hangers—they'll stretch down and out—fold them and put them in a drawer.

NOT EVERY DAY, BUT OFTEN:

Take a long, hot bath at least once a week to soak out dirt that quick showers often hit and miss.

Clip your fingernails and toenails short and straight across. Buy and learn to use a nail-clipper; don't round or shape your nails, and don't use anything on them except soap and water.

Shampoo your hair at least twice a week, using a good shampoo, not your bath soap, which lacks lather enough to get hair really clean; then rinse it thoroughly to get all the soap out.

If you won't cut your hair, at least have a barber shape and trim it every two weeks. Get used to telling him how you like your hair to look, and even if your mother is with you, be the one to pay the barber and give him the tip your parents suggested.

Avoid using sharp things, matches or hairpins, to clean your ears. Wash them seriously every time you bathe or shower, and nature will take it from there, doctors tell us.

Give your clothes a good brushing, especially around collars and shoulders of dark blazers and sports jackets. Use a flat brush instead of a whisk broom for more efficiency.

Learn to polish your shoes the right way: First, line up what you need: A soft cloth, a brush to buff with, a can of good shoe polish in the shade of your shoes, a can of lighter fluid, and a small amount of water. Now, with the cloth wrapped tightly around two fingers, wet it with lighter fluid and a dip of water. Then clean off all old wax and dirt before putting on a coat of polish. Let the polish dry a few seconds, then brush and buff to a good shine. For a spectacular finish, take a clean corner of the same cloth, dampen it with lighter fluid, dab it in the polish to pick up just enough for the tips of your shoes; that second coating applied with lighter fluid will give three times the shine when you buff it. Professionals finish with one last touch: they flick a few drops of water on the shoe tips, them give them a final buffing. They say the water "sets" the polish and keeps the shine longer.

HOW TO MAKE YOUR OWN BED

There's an old saying: "You made your bed—now lie in it." Any boy with class should make his own bed every morning; so as long as you're going to do it, you might as well do it right. The point is, you have to sleep in it every night, and there's a great difference between sleeping in a properly made bed and one that's messy.

Here's the way to do it if you use flat rather than contour sheets:

1. Center the bottom sheet lengthwise on the mattress, allowing a foot and a half (eighteen inches) for tucking under the head of the mattress to hold the sheet firm. There's no reason to tuck in the bottom end of this sheet because there isn't any pull under the feet.

2. Make a "square corner" at each side of the head of the bed like this: Take hold of the very edge of the sheet and raise it until it forms a straight line against the mattress, then let it fall back on the bed to form a right triangle.

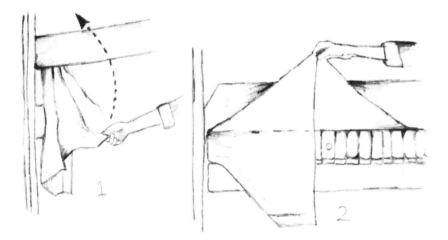

3. (a) Tuck the hanging part under the mattress. (b) Bring the triangle down over the side of the mattress, and (c) tuck the sheet smoothly under the mattress all the way down both sides of the bed.

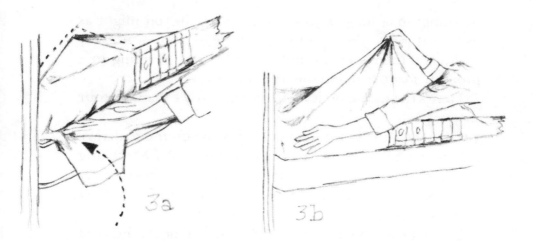

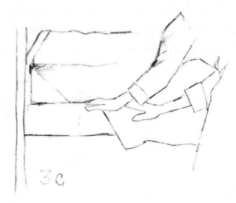

4. Center the top sheet lengthwise on the bed, leaving enough at the top to fold over a blanket, and about one foot at the bottom to tuck under the mattress. Make "square corners" at each side of the bottom, tucking the sheet under the mattress along each side.

5. Center the blanket lengthwise and tuck it under at the bottom, making the same "square corners" you made in the sheets. Fold the top sheet down over the blanket at the top.

6. Center the bedspread lengthwise but don't tuck it in all around. Just see that it hangs evenly on all sides. Plump up your bed pillow and center it under the top of the bedspread to keep it dust-free during the day.

PUTTING CLOTHES TOGETHER

Follow the customs of your school or community in choosing your clothes, then memorize a few tips men go by:

GOOD COLOR COMBINATIONS:

With a plaid or Madras or checked coat—a soft colored shirt; solid colored tie in the predominant shade of the coat; brown or black shoes.

With a brown sport coat or suit—White or cream-colored shirt; a gold, olive, tan, or dark red tie; brown shoes and socks.

With a dark blue suit or sport coat—White or light blue shirt; dark red, gold, or blue tie; black or navy socks; black shoes.

With a gray sport coat or suit—White, light blue, or gray shirt; dark red, olive, gold, or black tic; black shoes and socks.

With an olive sport coat or suit—White or cream-colored shirt; olive, black, or gold tie; black or brown shoes and socks.

With sport jackets—Gray, black, or olive pants.

BUY GOOD TIES AND LEARN TO TIE THEM PROPERLY

Wool ties tie neatly. To tie a tie: First step—turn up your

collar. Leave the top button of your shirt unbuttoned until you finish. Don't tie the knot too small or too tight.

Windsor knots have a broad knot and are good with wide-spread collars. Start with wide end of tie on your right, and extending a foot below narrow end:

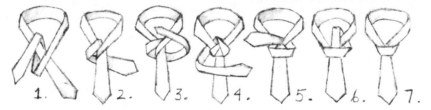

Half-windsor or four-in-hand knots look good with button-down collars: Start with the wide end of the tie on your right and extending a foot longer than the narrow end:

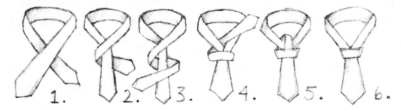

To finish: Tighten knot as you would a slip-knot, by holding narrow end and sliding knot up tight against the collar. Actually, the name four-in-hand comes from the slip-knot ties first worn by drivers of four-horse carriages! *Untie a tie to remove it.* Don't leave a knot in the tie when you hang it up.

THE BEST COLORS FOR YOU

If your hair is brown—wear grays, tans, and browns, but not very dark browns. Blues are also good. Stick to white or light colored shirts, not dark tones.

If your hair is red—wear warm browns, grays, and gray-greens. Stay away from yellows and oranges. Blue and green are your best accessory colors.

If your hair is light—wear dark blue, blue-grays, blue-greens, and reddish browns. If your skin is also fair, avoid colorless or pale tones; they'll make you look sick. In shirts, stay with light tones, with emphasis on pale blue.

If your hair is black—Dark gray is your best suit color, with a medium brown or a deep blue second. Stick to white or blue shirts, even though you can wear deep maroon shades better than redheads or fair haired boys can.

If you are short or plump—Wear single-breasted sports coats or suit jackets with the lapel that rolls down to the button at the waist. Buy them in dark solid colors. Avoid plaid jackets and bright colors.

If your face is full—You look best in pointed collar styles.

If your face is thin—You look best in a spread or rolled collar style.

If your skin is sallow—Avoid greens, yellows, and tans.

If your skin is dark—You can wear any color, but it's wise to avoid a combination of black and dark shades unless you don't mind looking like a gangster.

You'll hear a lot of talk about "black tie" which means a tuxedo, often called a dinner jacket, for evening wear. Boys under sixteen should not wear one. Instead, a dark blue suit is the proper attire for formal occasions.

The only jewelry a boy under sixteen should wear is a wrist watch and a simple tie bar.

HOW TO BUY A SUIT

When you go to a department store to shop for a suit, take your time, don't be rushed, or you may end up spending a lot of money for something you don't even like.

Try to dress up a bit when you shop by wearing the same type of shirt, belt, and shoes you'll be wearing with the new suit. This will help you get not only a better fit but also better service. The salesclerk is bound to take you less seriously if you come dressed in faded jeans, a heavy wool shirt, and sneakers.

Ask the salesclerk to show you all the suits available in your size. If you find a suit or suits that you like, check the workmanship before you make a final decision. Check for things like: the stitching—it should be neat, even, and reinforced in places such as behind the collar and at the armholes; the lining—it should be sewn securely enough to stand up to dry cleaning; the buttonholes—the stitching should be neat and secure; the buttons—they should be sewn on securely and they should all be there; the pattern (if there is one)—it should be joined and matched properly at all the seams.

Since no one looks good in a wrinkled suit, check the fabric by crumpling it in your hand. If the wrinkles remain, it's probably a good idea to look for a different suit.

Don't be surprised if you can't find a perfectly fitting suit right on the rack. Most suits need fitting, and you shouldn't pass up a nice suit just because the sleeves are too long or there's a bulge in the back—these things can be fixed. In better clothing stores the cost of fitting a suit is usually included in the price; in other stores there's an extra fee—just ask the clerk.

If your suit needs alterations, have the pants fitted first. Put them on with your belt and the shoes you'll be wearing with the suit. Starting at the top, the waist should fall slightly above the navel and be level to the ground all the way around. If the material buckles under your belt, the pants are too loose and should be taken in. Pants are too tight if you can't fit the flat of your hand comfortably between the waistband and your stomach.

The next area is the seat, which should fit smoothly and be comfortable when you stand and sit. If changes are required, have the fitter pin them. Otherwise, you won't be able to tell how the pant legs will fall, and they may come out too long or too short.

Pant legs should break in front and be one-half to three-quarters of an inch longer in the back. If you wear cuffs, these should hang level to the ground all the way around.

After the pants are fitted, fit the vest (if there is one) and the jacket. The jacket should feel comfortable when you stand, sit, and move around. Always swing your arms to see if the shoulders pull. Check for wrinkles and bulges in the neck, shoulder, and lapel areas—these can be taken in. Check for proper length by standing straight with your arms at your sides. If the bottom of the jacket fits into the curl of your fingers, it's the correct length.

The drawings on the next two pages will give you an idea of how a properly fitting suit should look.

CHECK-POINTS FOR THE RIGHT LOOK

The jacket should sit comfortably on your shoulders without hiking up in the back. The collar should hug the back of your neck. If there is a slight give in the collar, try a small alteration or a proper pressing.

Your jacket should always cover the seat of your pants. It should be long enough to rest in the bend of your fingers when you cup your hand at your side.

In a two-button jacket the bottom button should be at belt level. In a three-button suit the middle button should be at belt level.

Whether you get your pants cuffed is up to you—a matter of taste. Generally, cuffs look better on sportier clothes and should be about two inches deep.

One-half inch of the shirt collar should show above the collar of the jacket.

The sleeve of the jacket should end at the middle of your wrist bone when your arm is hanging at your side.

One-half inch of the shirt sleeve should be shown below the jacket sleeve when your arm is held down.

Pants should fall straight when you are standing and should not bag in the seat or the crotch. Also, your pants should break slightly in front where they touch the shoe; in back, they should drop to the top of the heel.

right   wrong

The coat collar should hug your neck at the back and sides. Otherwise, you'll have a horse-collar effect.

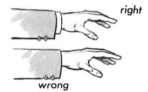

right

wrong

One-half inch of the shirt sleeve should show below the jacket sleeve when your arm is held down.

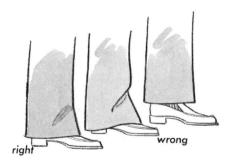

right   wrong

Try to avoid a sloppy break in your pant legs. Pants should just touch the tops of your shoes in front and fall slightly longer in back.

Table Manners

When man first made his appearance on earth, he ate with his hands, which were his only utensils. It wasn't easy to eat animals that way, so as soon as man learned to cook his food with fire (nobody knows how long he ate his meat raw), he invented utensils. First he invented the bowl, to drink from; then the platter to put his food on; then someone—we'll never know who it was—thought of inventing a spoon, then a knife, and finally some bright person came up with the idea of the fork. (The teaspoon was invented after tea was discovered.)

With each new utensil invented came instructions as to how they should be used. Therefore, table manners are no more than the correct way to use the tools of the table.

Centuries ago in Japan a man could be executed for not having the proper table manners. Our culture doesn't execute anyone, but it does frown on people who don't know how to eat properly.

Actually the real reason for good table manners is this: You don't make a mess of things and cause everyone else at the table to lose his appetite.

THE TABLE AND ITS TOOLS

The best cooks in the world are men, and the best servers are waiters. Therefore, it's up to the male to know the tools of eating, and where they belong on a table.

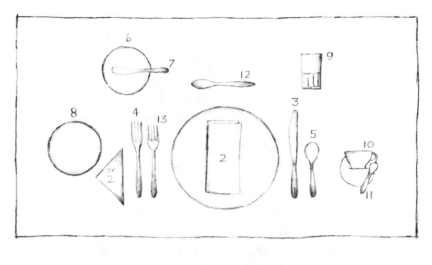

1. The Plate	7. The Butter Knife
2. The Napkin	8. The Salad Plate
3. The Knife	9. The Glass
4. The Fork	10. The Cup and Saucer
5. The Spoon	11. The Coffee Spoon
6. The Bread-and-Butter Plate	12. The Dessert Spoon
	13. The Salad Fork

BEFORE YOU TAKE A BITE

A boy should come to the table with washed hands, combed hair, and a reasonably clean shirt. He waits for the hostess to sit down before he does. At home his mother may be considered the hostess, but if she's serving the dinner he may have to start before his mother gets a chance to sit down. It's good practice at home to hold the chair for his mother or sister, but some sisters could resent it. The proper method for helping a woman sit down is to gently pull out the chair, and then while she is half-seated, push

it in under her. Timing is everything, and if you push too soon or too late there could be an accident.

When everyone is seated, you wait to see if "Grace" is going to be said. You don't pick up your napkin until the blessing is over. If there is no blessing, the hostess will pick up her napkin; then you can pick up yours and place it across your lap.

You wait until the hostess or your mother begins to eat. At small dinner parties people wait until everyone is served.

FEEDING YOUR FACE

Soup is eaten from the side of a soup spoon which is oval-shaped and larger than a teaspoon. The whole spoon never goes into the mouth, but is tilted to let the liquid flow in. When the soup bowl or plate is nearly empty, it can be tipped away from the person so the last spoonsful can be eaten—without scraping!

Sometimes a clear soup will be served in cups. Then the spoon is used for the first few tastes until the soup is cool enough to drink directly from the cup. Both hands are used to hold the cup.

Soup spoons are always put on the plate, not left in the bowl, when the soup is finished.

Crackers are put on the plate under the soup bowl, or on the bread-and-butter plate. Large crackers should be broken in two like rolls or bread, never crumpled or thrown into soup. Oyster crackers, however, may be put into soup a few at a time.

Fish is eaten with a fish fork and a specially shaped knife, wide at the top, blunt-edged, and with a small curve at the end for opening the main bone. The fish knife is held in the right hand between thumb and index finger (different from the way the meat knife is held) to cut the fish and

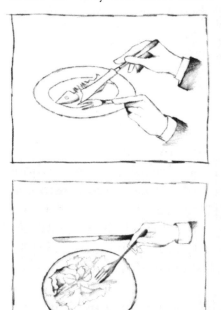

push it up on the back of the fork. The fork is held in the left hand with prongs down. Fish can also be eaten with the fork alone— in the right hand, of course —and in this case, the knife is left on the table.

Salads should be eaten with a fork only, but when there is a thick wedge of lettuce it is just as correct to use both a knife and fork. When salad is a separate course, a salad fork (wider and shorter than a dinner fork) is used; and it is left on the salad plate when finished. At lunch, salad is often served at the same time as the main course. Then the regular dinner fork is used.

Sandwiches are finger foods in most cases, but they should always be cut or broken into halves or fourths before they're tackled at the table.

Spaghetti is not eaten in mid-air, nor is it cut up on the plate except for infants. The best way is to twist a small amount around the fork, using a large spoon in the other hand to twist against, and then hope it doesn't unwind on its way to the mouth.

Celery and olives are eaten with the fingers, and olive pits are removed from the mouth with the fingers then put on the bread-and-butter plate or the edge of the dinner plate. *Buffets are fun* because everyone helps himself. There are no special rules about approaching the buffet table except that a boy should let a girl precede him, of course. Usually a stack of empty plates shows where a person is to start. Knives, forks, and napkins will be next to the plates—or at the very end of the food line-up—in either case, it's important not to forget to pick them up. Unless a table has been set for everyone at the party, guests are free to eat wherever they're comfortable. A boy offers to refill a girl's plate for her.

When refreshments are in a punchbowl, a boy offers to serve a girl. He uses the ladle to dip into the punch and pour cups half-full. It's best to carry out this maneuver over the bowl to avoid dripping on the tablecloth.

AH, THE COMFORT OF DOING THINGS RIGHT!

A napkin is picked up by the left hand and placed on the lap. It is unfolded half-way when it is a large dinner size, or all the way when it is a small luncheon one. It is not tucked into a belt, collar, or between shirt buttons except on a very small child. A napkin is used primarily to remove food from lips and fingers before drinking from a glass or cup. It is best to lift a corner of a large napkin rather than the whole thing. At the end of a meal, the napkin is not folded again. Instead, it is replaced on the table to the left of the plate. It can be slightly crumpled together, but should not be rolled into a messy ball. Neither should paper napkins, which have the same rules as fine linen ones.

A knife is used for cutting meat, one piece at a time. It is held in the right hand with the handle in the palm and the index finger along the back of the blade to steady it. It is never used in the left hand, except by a left-handed person. After the knife is used, it should never again be placed on the table, or even balanced with the handle on the table and the blade on the edge of the plate. When the knife is not in use, it is placed in the upper right-hand part of the plate, the handle to the right, the blade on the plate, not along the edge. When a boy has finished eating, he puts his knife and fork side-by-side on the plate with their handles toward the lower side of the plate. The knife goes outside the fork with its cutting edge toward the center of the plate.

A fork is used in the right hand when eating. The only time it goes in the left hand is when it is being used to hold something for cutting. Then, the handle rests in the palm and the index finger extends along the back of the fork to hold in place whatever is being cut. After meat is cut, the fork is then transferred to the right hand for eating. This is called the Zig-Zag or Criss-Cross method (in contrast to the Continental method of many European countries, where the fork is kept in the left hand for eating). During the meal, when the fork is not in use, it is placed on the plate, tines up, with the handle to the right.

All spoons are held in the right hand. The soup spoon has a few additional rules of its own: Only the side is put to the lips, then tipped slightly so the liquid flows into the mouth. The entire spoon is not put in the mouth. After stirring coffee, tea, cocoa, etc. a spoon should be placed on the saucer, never left in the cup or put on the table. Exception: A long-handled spoon may be left in a tall glass of iced tea, for instance, when no saucer is provided.

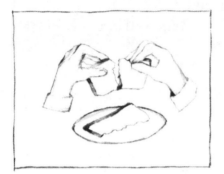

A butter knife is used to spread butter, jam, or jelly on bread, biscuits, rolls, and toast *after* they have been broken into smaller mouthful-size pieces with the fingers. You never butter a whole slice of bread, or even cut a biscuit or muffin, with this knife. And it is not to be used to take butter from the main dish, which will have its own knife. Bread to be buttered is held *on* the bread-and-butter plate, not in the palm of the hand. When there is no butter knife a regular one may be used. It's an interesting side rule that the fork, not a knife, is used to put butter on vegetables and jellies on meats.

The butter plate also serves as the place to put radishes, olives, and celery when they are served. Jellies and gravies are put alongside the food they go with on the dinner plate. Who knows why, but salted nuts are put directly on the tablecloth; so are little after-dinner candies that come in ruffled papers. You pick up both candy and paper at the same time and put them on the table beside your plate.

ADDITIONAL SILVER TO RECOGNIZE

A salad fork is shorter and stubbier than a dinner fork and is used for either salad or dessert. When salad is served after the main course, as it is in most cases, the salad fork will

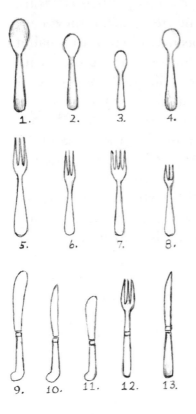

1. Dessert or cereal spoon; also used for soup served in a bowl or soup plate.
2. Teaspoon; used for regular coffee cups, tea and small desserts.
3. After-dinner coffee spoon.
4. Round-bowl soup spoon.
5 Dinner fork.
6. Smaller fork is used for lunch, salad, dessert.
7. Salad or dessert fork, with broader first tine for cutting.
8. Oyster fork; also used for crab meat, lobster, shrimp.
9. Dinner knife.
10. Steak knife; has a short, very sharp blade—often serrated—and long handle.
11. Flat-bladed butter knife.
12. Fruit fork; usually has three tines.
13. Fruit knife; has sharp steel blade.

be placed on the left of the plate, inside the dinner fork. When salad is a first course at family or informal meals, the salad fork is placed outside the dinner fork. When there is no salad course, this fork is used for dessert and is usually placed on the dessert plate or above the dinner plate along with the dessert spoon.

A dessert spoon is longer and slightly larger than a teaspoon. It is usually placed on the dessert plate, but it may be placed on the table at the beginning of an informal meal.

The serving fork and spoon are larger than regular forks and spoons and are placed on a platter or in a vegetable dish. When serving yourself, hold them like any fork and spoon: with your right hand, slip the spoon under a portion of food; then, holding the food in place with the fork, transfer it to your plate. Replace the serving fork and spoon tines and face down after you have served yourself.

Demitasse (Means one-half cup) *cups and spoons* are small, after-dinner cups of coffee, served with miniature spoons about four inches long which are usually placed on the saucer when coffee is served.

A finger bowl is often provided near the end of a meal, for the simple purpose of rinsing tips of fingers after eating buttery or sticky foods (corn on the cob, lobster, fresh fruit, etc.). The finger bowl usually appears on a small plate or saucer with a doily. The finger bowl, together with the saucer or plate and the doily, should be lifted and placed on the left of the dessert plate. Only the tips of fingers are dipped in the water. Both hands may be dipped, but it should be a brief action, not a showy one. When a dessert spoon and fork come along with the finger bowl, you place them where they belong: the spoon on the right of the dessert plate, the fork on the left.

A book of boo-boos could probably be written about the people who have drunk the water in their finger bowls; so no boy should worry if he has to peek at the hostess and follow what she does throughout the whole routine.

FOODS THAT TAKE A LITTLE TALENT

Sometimes you're served food that looks so mysterious you half wish it came with instructions for eating—at least the first time. Then again, other foods are such old favorites it's a surprise to find there are more grown-up ways to handle them. It's sad, but there are fewer and fewer finger foods as you leave childhood.

Never let far-out foods scare you. You'll rarely run into more than one at a time, and if you're up a tree about how to tackle something new just say, "I've never eaten this before. . . ." and you'll quickly get advice from your hostess or another guest.

Look over this list; then when you come face-to-face with something like snails, at least you can say you've read about them:

SEAFOOD

Shrimp cocktail—Each shrimp is eaten in one bite if the shrimp is small. If it's jumbo size, you can eat it in two bites from the seafood fork. Put the fork on the plate under the seafood dish when you're finished.

Oysters and clams in open shells are usually served on a plate of cracked ice with a seafood fork alongside it. Hold the shell in place with one hand, and with the other lift the whole oyster or clam out of the shell and eat it in one bite. Don't pick up the shell itself, even at the end to get those few drops of juice. Seafood sauce is usually served in a small bowl placed right in the middle of the ice; so dip each piece in it before eating. Put oyster crackers on your butter plate or on the tablecloth.

Steamed clams are a different story: with your fingers, lift out each clam by its neck, then pull the body from it and **discard the neck part. Dip the clam in melted butter and** eat it in one bite. Because clams usually leave sand in the cooking broth, you will often be served a separate cup of strained broth to drink. Special note: If a clam shell hasn't opened during the cooking, don't pry it open. Put it aside and forget about it. The closed shell means it shouldn't be eaten.

Snails are served in their own shells on a special plate with dents to hold each shell upright. That's because snails are cooked with a buttery garlic sauce which you sip from the shell after you've eaten the snail. First, with your left hand, pick up and hold a shell with your napkin (snails are always h-o-t) or with the special metal clamps usually served with snails. Then with your right hand dig out the snail with a seafood fork and eat it in one bite. If you don't want to sip the liquid from the shell, you can dip small pieces of bread in it with your fork.

Lobsters are a man-sized job, but worth every bit of the struggle. Luckily they're always served with a tool that looks like a nutcracker. You use it to crack the two big claws. Then you break them apart further with both hands. Next, pick up one claw and with the seafood fork dig out the meat and put it on your plate to cut into bite-sized pieces. Finally, dip it in melted butter and get your reward for all the work. To get meat out of the small claws, break them with your fingers and either suck out the meat or dig it out with your fork. The coral-colored roe of the lobster and the soft green liver are both eaten with a fork—and they're delicious. One caution: Lobsters are cooked in boiling water; so be careful of steam when you first crack them open.

MEATS

Fried chicken is eaten with a knife and fork unless you're at a picnic or a drive-in where no forks are supplied. Steady the piece of chicken on your plate with your fork in your left hand; then with the right hand cut away the meat a bite at a time. It takes a bit of whittling.

Chops of any kind—pork, veal, lamb—are eaten with a knife and fork; never be caught picking one up with your hands.

Barbecued spare ribs are finger food. Pick them up and nibble away. You'd leave the table hungry and frustrated if you tried to use a knife and fork; there's too little meat on each bone.

Frogs' legs, like any tiny-boned meat, can be eaten partly with a knife and fork, partly with fingers—otherwise you'd miss most of the meat. First, sever the frog's leg at the joint and eat as much meat as you can cut off the larger part with your knife and fork. When you come to the smaller part of the leg, it's perfectly okay to put it into your mouth and remove the meat this way. Put the bones back on the side of your plate.

VEGETABLES

Artichokes are eaten with fingers most of the way. Pull off one leaf at a time and dip it into melted butter or sauce, then pull it through your teeth to get just the soft part at the very end of the leaf—the rest is too tough. When all the outer leaves are finished and arranged neatly on the side of your plate, remove the "choke," which is the fuzzy part in the middle of the artichoke, by cutting under it and lifting it off. Then cut the artichoke heart into pieces, dipping each piece into sauce with your fork.

Asparagus is not eaten with the fingers; it's too messy. Eat the soft tips with your fork only, then cut the tender part of the stem with your knife and fork.

Baked potatoes should not be scooped out onto your plate and mashed; they should be eaten out of the potato shell. Use your fork to put butter on the potato as you mash your way along. At the end, cut up the skin with your knife and fork and eat it for an extra dose of iron!

French fried potatoes are eaten with a fork after being cut into shorter lengths if necessary. Don't spear a piece and bite away at it from your fork. Of course, at a drive-in or on a picnic, French fries are definitely finger food.

Corn on the cob is a both-hands food. When you're served, take an ear from the platter with your fingers unless tongs are provided. Put it on your main plate, not on the butter plate. Use your butter knife to spread butter on one or two rows at a time, never on the whole ear at once or it will run down your arms. Lift the corn to your mouth with both hands and nibble away "typewriter style," not around-and-around; again to avoid the drips. Some people like to cut corn off the cob at the table, but it's a risky proposition, and you'd need more than a finger bowl to clean up after the operation.

Peas are eaten with a fork, not a spoon, using the fork like a shovel to spear and scoop them up. Don't mix peas with your mashed potatoes to rush the job. Anyone who's chased peas around his plate is bound to admire the skill with which English people slide peas up onto the back of their forks, then wedge a small piece of meat or potato against them to keep them from rolling off on the trip up to the mouth!

FRUITS

Grapefruit is eaten with a regular teaspoon or a pointed grapefruit spoon. Take seeds out of your mouth with your spoon. Don't pick up the shell and squeeze out the last drops of juice even if that's the best part.

Melons: Cantaloupe wedges are eaten with either a dessert spoon or with a knife and fork. Melon balls are eaten with a spoon. Watermelon served in wedges is eaten with a fork, or with both knife and fork. You cut away the seed part before you put each piece into your mouth, but if a seed gets into your mouth anyway, the best way to remove it is with your fingers.

Peaches are first cut with a knife and fork, then eaten with the fingers or with a knife and fork. A small peach should be cut in half; a large one in several pieces. Don't polish the peach fuzz or try to remove it with your napkin. At picnics, eat peaches like Adam and Eve and forget about juice stains!

Bananas served whole at the table should be peeled half-way or all the way, the skin put aside on your plate, then the banana eaten by breaking off pieces with your fingers or cutting them off with your knife and fork. Avoid the monkey method of chomping away at a half-peeled banana with the skin draped down over your hand.

Apples and pears at the table are cut into quarters, then the seeds or cores are removed with your knife and fork. From there on you can eat with your fingers or fork.

Tangerines are peeled, then one segment at a time is broken off and eaten—preferably in two bites—with the fingers.

Oranges are peeled spirally in one fell swoop if you're a master at it, then eaten segment by segment with the fingers.

Grapes are cut or broken off in small clusters from the main bunch, put on the dessert plate, and eaten from there.

Don't pick off one grape at a time from the main dish. Put seeds on the side of your plate with your fingers.

Fresh strawberries are picked up by the hulls (stem plus a few little leaves) and dipped in whatever is served with them—sugar, whipped cream, or sour cream—and eaten with the fingers. Berries in juice are always eaten with a spoon.

Lemon slices on your meat or fish are not picked up. To get the juice out, press the slice with your fork. However, a wedge of lemon *is* picked up and squeezed or pressed against the prongs of a fork to let the juice trickle out.

ETCETERA

Celery should be broken in at least two pieces, never eaten a whole stalk at a time. Put celery on your butter plate if you have one; on the main plate, if not. Never dip your celery in a salt dish; instead put some salt on the plate beside the celery.

Olives belong on the butter or salad plate, but if neither is provided, put them on your dinner plate. Eat an olive with two or three bites, holding it with your fingers. Never plop a whole olive into your mouth.

Pizza is not held flat in the palm of the hand. Instead, thumb on the bottom, two fingers around the edge, bend the wedge so the point goes up toward your mouth.

Sandwiches when served with a knife and fork are usually extra-thick or extra-complicated, so eat them with the knife and fork exactly as you would a piece of meat, a bite at a time.

Chinese food tastes twice as exotic when you eat it with chopsticks, but if you haven't learned how to use them, ask for a fork the first time. Then all the best things won't be gone by the time you've picked up twelve grains of rice.

Crackers are not broken into your soup unless you're eating alone in the kitchen. Put them on your butter plate or on the plate under the soup bowl.

Cookies are taken from the main serving plate with your fingers and put on your plate, not directly into your mouth. Eat a small cookie in one bite, but break a larger one into two pieces. When cookies are served with ice cream, put them on the edge of the dessert plate, not on the tablecloth.

Candy in paper frills is picked up paper and all—otherwise the plate would be half-filled with "empties." Put both candy and paper on the tablecloth beside your plate until you're ready to eat it. Don't pop the candy into your mouth while you're still holding the paper.

Toothpicks were meant to be used in private, not at the table or during dinner. Consider toothpicks as a substitute for dental floss or your toothbrush—then you'll know what to do with them and when.

HOW TO PROPOSE A TOAST

Toasting another person is the highest honor you can pay him. When you raise a glass (in your case it will probably be Coca-Cola; later on it will be wine or liquor), and say "Cheers" or "To your health," it means that you and he are friends and you're drinking together in comradely spirit. Every nation has its toast. The French say "Bon

Santé," the Scandinavians say "Skoal," the Israelis say "L'Chaim," and in pubs all over Great Britain they say, " 'Ere's mud in your eye."

Drinking to someone you want to praise or honor goes back to the days of Julius Caesar, but it was the early English who gave us the word "toast." Sitting around an open fire, men dropped a piece of toasted bread into a glass of wine, then drank until the glass was empty of everything but the little piece of toast. Naturally they drank a lot of wine that way; so today we usually just sip from a glass when we are toasting someone.

Also in those days, they used to smash their glasses on the stones of the fireplace after they'd toasted a woman or a very special person—to prevent the glass from ever being used again for less sacred reasons. We don't smash glasses today, but you may occasionally hear about bachelor dinners where they revive the old ritual by breaking very cheap glasses (which someone has bought for just this reason) after the groom-to-be and his pals have toasted the girl he's going to marry the next day.

As you grow older, toasts take on more importance, and in some cases require a short statement in praise of the honored guest. You think of something nice about the person being feted—or about the host or hostess—then you rise to your feet and with your glass in hand you make your statement (always favorable, of course, and always brief). At the end you say, "And therefore I propose a toast to my dear friend Ezra who rode all the way from Grizzly to Maverick without once getting car-sick." Then you raise your glass to eye-level, wait for others to stand, and you sip a little of the liquid. You hold a wineglass by the lower part of the bowl with your little finger on the stem to steady it.

The only time you don't join in a toast is when you are the one being toasted. Then you sit there and blush. When the toast is over, you either nod your head as a thank-you or you stand up and say a few words of thanks. You don't drink from your own glass until all the others have done so, or you'd be drinking to yourself.

Informal toasts can also be proposed and drunk without standing up, but it's rude *not* to join in a toast at all. So if you don't want to drink, at least raise the glass to your lips and pretend. Also, there's an old superstition that it's bad luck to toast someone with plain water, but everything else goes: orange juice, milk, ginger ale (looks the most like champagne), even iced tea.

It might be a good idea to practice toasts by getting up at the dinner table after each meal and toasting your father or mother. The more practice you have on your feet the better it will be for you when you grow up, because toasts are a man's job. Say, "To my mother—the greatest cook in Hillsboro; I would like to toast her for this fine roast beef." Or: "To my father, a man of great charity and warmth, who will, I'm sure, allow me to go to the movies tomorrow afternoon."

Girls and women never rise after they've been toasted unless they're going to make a speech in answer. They just sit there and smile their thanks.

Sometimes a toast is made to the President of the United States to honor him even though he isn't there. In this case, it will always be the first toast of the evening. At other times, a governor, a mayor, or a dignitary will be toasted as one of the guests, but unless it is part of the planned program, he will simply nod his head in acknowledgment and will not stand up or speak.

HOW TO BE INVITED BACK AGAIN
FOR MEALS

• *Sit up straight at the table* with your chest a few inches away from the table edge. Lean forward slightly when you bring food up to your mouth; then if anything drops, it will land on the plate, not on your shirt.

• *Take part in table conversation.* You don't have to entertain or give reports, but listen and try to contribute to the talk; then everyone will enjoy having you there. Avoid unpleasant topics about health, accidents, the cost of the food you're eating, or personal feuds with other members of the family.

• *When you pass your plate for a second helping,* put your knife and fork side-by-side; and far enough from the edge of the plate so they won't fall off.

• *Before talking or drinking from the glass,* chew and swallow all the food in your mouth, then wipe your lips with your napkin.

• *Chew your food without noise and without smacking your lips,* even if it's your favorite dish. The secret of this talent is to put on your fork only the amount of food your mouth can accommodate. It's very uncomfortable to chew on an over-sized piece of meat until it's whittled down to swallowing size.

• *Keep your elbows off the table while eating.* Between courses, it's perfectly okay to rest your elbows on the table, but not to lounge.

• *Don't circle a plate with your arm* as if the Indians were attacking!

• *Don't use your own spoon, fork, or knife to serve yourself from main dishes* such as the sugar bowl, the butter dish, the chop platter, or the vegetable dish.

• *Don't lean on the chairs next to you,* and don't tilt back on your own—it could be a fragile antique on its last legs.

• *Don't reach across the table or in front of another person.* Just ask to have the food passed by mentioning the name of the person you are asking—otherwise, everyone at the table has to stop and look for what you want.

• *When you are being served,* you don't have to say thank you to a waiter or a maid. You never take the whole dish or platter that is being offered, but simply serve yourself a portion using the serving spoon and fork in the dish. Then you put them back on the platter or dish with the fork on the bottom and the spoon, face down, over the fork. You can expect to be served from your left side, and to have plates removed from your right side. You don't have to greet the maid serving you unless you know her well, then a cheery "Hello, Mary" is more than welcome.

• *Don't eat and run.*

• *At the end of dinner,* wait to be excused before you leave the table. If you must leave the table before the end of the meal for personal reasons, don't give excuses, simply say, "Please excuse me" or "May I please be excused?" Then leave your napkin, slightly crumpled, beside your plate on the table, not on the seat of your chair.

• *At parties or larger dinners,* wait for the hostess to signal that the meal is over by putting down her napkin and rising. No one is supposed to do either one before she does.

• *If a woman or girl leaves the table briefly during dinner,* only the man or boy on her left rises to help her with her chair; and it's usually only a half-rise as a courteous gesture.

• *Leave your plate where it is when you have finished eating.* Don't push it in toward the center of the table. In fact, don't rearrange any dishes on the table with the exception of the fingerbowl served on the dessert plate.

• *In leaving the table,* help the same girl or woman you seated at the beginning of the meal. Stand behind her chair, then pull it back gently as she slides out from the right side.

Traveling

You'll probably travel a lot during your lifetime—perhaps even to the moon on business some day. Until you go away to school, however, you'll usually be traveling with your parents or someone older. But this is as good a time as any to learn some basic "rules of the road," then when you're ready to travel alone they'll be familiar to you.

Wherever you're going, write down the departure and arrival times of your train, plane, or bus. Put name tags on each piece of luggage. If your luggage is a popular color or fabric, paste a seal of some kind on it so you can spot yours easily when you go to claim it at the end of the trip. All luggage except a small hand piece must be checked. On a plane or bus it is checked just as you depart. For a long train ride, you may check luggage ahead of time.

When you're old enough to carry your own money, you'll understand that it's better and safer to carry American Express travelers' checks instead of cash. They are issued in checks of $10, $20, $50, or $100. You pay $1 for each $100 you buy of them. Travelers' checks are signed when you purchase them and again when you cash them.

WHEN YOU TRAVEL BY PLANE

The only people you tip are the porters who carry your luggage from the airport entrance to the check-out counter,

and, when you get off a plane, from the baggage claim counter to your transportation away from the airport. On planes your bags are checked in. You don't have to worry about them until the end of your trip. Only the smallest piece that can fit under the seat may be carried aboard the plane.

Reservations are made either First Class, Coach, Economy Tour, or Thrift Class. There is a considerable amount of difference in the fares. First class is seated in the forward section of the plane, separated from the rest of the cabin. First class seats are roomier, and the meals are more elaborate. Fewer and fewer people travel first class these days, since jet travel is so fast.

You must always arrive thirty minutes before your plane is scheduled to depart. As soon as you arrive at the airport, you check the gate from which your flight will leave by looking at the gate numbers posted behind the ticket counter. Your flight will also be announced over a loud speaker. If your flight is delayed, you will be given free meals; if your flight is cancelled, you will be given free overnight hotel accommodations. Therefore, don't be afraid to ask for these privileges in such emergencies.

Your seat number is attached to the outside of your plane ticket. You show them both to the stewardess when you board the plane. The stewardess will check your coat for you and hang it up.

Pillow and blankets are on a rack above your seat if you need them. Don't tip your seat back without first checking to see if the person behind you is using the tray on the back of your seat. The "Fasten Seat Belt" sign is at the front of the plane.

There is a button on the overhead panel to call the stewardess if you need her. If you get pressure on your eardrums when you're going up or landing, yawn or pretend to chew gum—either one will help relieve "stuffy ears." A ventilator is above your seat in case you need more air, and there is an empty paper bag in the pocket of the seat if you need it. Men's and women's toilets are not marked separately. They are called wash rooms and have a sign that flashes when they are occupied. Meals are served at no fee. You never tip an airline stewardess, but you do say thank you when you leave the plane. To claim your bags, you usually wait about ten minutes for them to be unloaded. then you show your check stubs (stapled to your ticket) for identification of your own luggage. If there is no one handling baggage, just pick up your bags and leave.

WHEN YOU TRAVEL BY TRAIN

You tip porters 25¢ a bag, 50¢ for large ones. If you're going by Pullman, take a small overnight bag with you, and either check large pieces of luggage ahead of time or ask the porter to store them for you at the end of the car in the space provided for them.

In the dining car you are often seated with other people. The headwaiter seats you, but you do not tip him. You write down your order on a slip of paper that will be given to you. You tip your waiter fifteen percent of the bill, but if you order just a sandwich and a Coke, never leave less than 25¢.

The porter makes up your berth if you're traveling by Pullman. You wash and get ready for bed in the men's room, but you get into your night clothes in your own berth. The hammock on the wall is for your clothes. You tip the Pullman porter $1 a night.

When you have a while to wait before your train leaves, you can check your baggage in a locker. To use a locker, drop a coin in first—usually a dime or a quarter—place your baggage inside, and take the locker key with you.

When you travel by coach, you do not have to reserve a seat in most cases. Parlor or chair cars are reserved, however. Pullman means that you are given a berth. In the daytime, this section becomes two double seats facing each other. A reservation for lower berth means that you get the seat facing forward. The porter makes up your berth when you want to go to bed. The upper berth is reached by a ladder. You undress in your berth or you wear your robe over your pajamas and go to the dressing room. Bathrooms are marked separately for men and women. When you leave your berth during the night, leave your curtain open and the light on so you can find your way back.

Porters can send telegrams for you, or call you at a special time in the morning. The porter adjusts the air conditioning for you, sets up the writing table, brushes off your coat, takes care of your luggage, and helps you off the train. He earns the $1 tip you give him.

The Vista-Dome is usually at the end of the train. It is equipped with comfortable chairs, radios, tables for writing, magazines, and newspapers.

Redcaps who carry your luggage are given 35¢ for each piece of luggage.

WHEN YOU TRAVEL BY BUS

When there are no toilets on the bus, it stops frequently for coffee breaks so this is generally no problem. In case of emergency, it's permissible to ask the bus driver to make a stop. Stops are also made for meals. It is perfectly correct to take your own lunch and eat it in your seat as long as you are neat about it and don't make a clutter with wrapping paper and orange rinds.

Usually the first passengers in line for a bus get the first choice of seats. The front pair of seats on the right are the best ones because you have a better view. Second best are in the center because they're not over the wheels. The seat you select when you board the bus is the one you keep throughout the trip. No one can claim it when you get out to make stops. But to avoid embarrassing people who are coming aboard at that stop, leave an article in the seat when you get out.

Keep your transistor radio low—it can be very annoying to other passengers.

You never tip a bus driver.

WHEN YOU TRAVEL BY SHIP

It is best to book passage months in advance. There are three classes of accommodations: First, Second (Cabin), and Third (Tourist). Cabin and tourist classes are the most fun and are preferred by young people. Cabin and tourist passengers can't visit the first class section except by invitation, but first class passengers have the run of the whole ship.

Arrive at least an hour before sailing time. The best cabins are outside cabins because they have portholes. Deck chairs are free on most ships. Check with the deck steward as soon as possible to reserve one. Ask him which spot on the ship is best for getting sun and for staying out of the wind. If it gets cool, steamer rugs will be provided by the deck steward. Never carry blankets or pillows from your own cabin. Everyone must run out for fire drills—fire is the single biggest nightmare of any ship.

Breakfast, lunch, and dinner—as well as snacks in the mid-morning or afternoon—are always served. Preference for early or late seating, or for a special location in the dining room, is made through the dining room steward or purser as soon as you board the ship. If you delay, you'll be given whatever seating is left over.

You give tips on the last day of your voyage. Officers or sailors are never tipped. You tip about ten percent of the price of your ticket, then this amount is evenly divided among the steward, stewardesses, maids, etc., who have given you personal service during the trip.

WHEN YOU STAY IN A HOTEL

THE BELLBOY

You can't pick up your key and go to your room by yourself; you wait until the bellboy gets your room key from the desk clerk, picks up your bag, and takes you to the elevator and to your room. He checks the air-conditioning, turns on the bathroom light, and opens the closet doors. You tip him 25¢ for each bag he carried and an extra 25¢ for opening up the room. He's never given less than 50¢ under any circumstances. When you are checking out of the hotel, a bellboy comes up to your room and takes your luggage down to the lobby. You again tip him 25¢ per bag, but not for checking you out of your room.

ROOM SERVICE

When you have food served in your room you tip the same fifteen percent as in a restaurant. You give this tip to the waiter directly, or add it to the bill when you sign it. Food bills are then added to your hotel bill.

VALET SERVICE

You give the valet who picks up clothes to be pressed at least 25¢. He will return them to your room, even if you're not there, when they're pressed.

MAIDS

If you stay in a hotel more than one night, leave $1 for each night in an envelope marked "for the maid."

When you are ready to leave, you turn in your key at the desk and pay your bill at the cashier's window. The same bellboy who brought your luggage to the lobby should then load the car, and he is tipped 25¢ per bag at that time. You don't tip him twice for bringing bags to the lobby and to the car. You don't tip the doorman unless he's had a difficult time getting you a taxi.

House Guesting

It's usually a fine adventure to spend the weekend or just to "sleep over" at a friend's house, even if he lives nearby. It's a compliment to you when you're invited, and means you're a special friend. But it doesn't mean you're free to run wild or abuse property or forget any of these good-sense rules about being someone's house guest:

First of all, make sure you know when you're supposed to arrive and how long you'll be expected to stay. Get this straight before you leave home so that everybody, including your own family, can make plans to accompany you to your friend's house and then call for you at the end of the visit.

When you're an overnight guest only, it's best to leave at the end of the morning next day — no later than noon, and before lunch time.

Take your own toilet necessities with you so you won't have to borrow personal things like a hair brush or comb. When packing your overnight bag, think of everything you normally use or need at home in a twenty-four-hour period; then as you mentally picture the routine, put each needed item in your suitcase.

As a guest of someone else's family, you'll be expected to follow their way of doing things with no comment on

85

how differently you may do things at home. After all, it's fun to see how other people live; and it might give you a new idea or two. Usually everyone in the house has a little more fun and freedom when there's a guest, but you'll still have to go along with whatever rules the family observes about mealtimes, bedtime, television viewing, and indoor play.

Unless you're invited to, you shouldn't help yourself to food from the kitchen or refrigerator whenever you're slightly hungry. If hunger pangs set in—and they always seem to when you're in a strange house—it's perfectly okay to say, "I'd like a little snack," or "I'm hungry for something; maybe a piece of bread and butter." No one wants you to wither away.

Your host or his parents will probably make plans for indoor or outdoor activities and for any special amusements; it's up to you to be a good sport and accept them.

Never open drawers, closets, or medicine cabinets merely to inspect their contents—they're all private property.

Make your own bed each morning if there isn't a maid to do it. When you leave at the end of a weekend stay, take the sheets off your bed and pull the bedspread up over the mattress or blankets.

When you're ready to leave, pack up everything you brought—so nothing will have to be mailed or returned to you—and then thank your host's mother for inviting you. If you've stayed overnight only, saying thank you is sufficient, but if your visit was out-of-town or for a weekend or longer, you must write to your friend's mother when you get home and thank her for having you. It's also thoughtful to send her a little gift. Your mother will help you select and mail one along with your thank-you letter.

When you are entertaining a house guest who is going to share your room, be sure to clear out some of your clothes in your closet and leave a few empty hangers so he can hang up his clothes. In the bathroom, he should be given his own towel, washcloth, soap, and drinking glass.

FRIENDLY VISITS

When you visit your friends, try to time it right. Don't drop in too early in the morning, too late at night, or right at mealtime. If you accidentally arrive when his family is eating, tell your friend you'll come back later, even if you have nothing better to do than to walk around the block a few times. Never barge into a house without knocking, even when you know the family well.

When you enter, pause a second and if someone doesn't offer to take your coat, say "Where should I put my coat?" Then wait until you're told where to sit down. When adults come in the room where you're sitting, stand up, say "Good evening" or "Hello," and shake hands.

When you want to leave, wait for the right moment to announce it. Don't jump up and leave while someone is talking. Shake hands and quietly say, "Good night" or "Goodbye." Your friend should help you find your coat, and walk to the door with you, giving you a chance to say, "Thanks, it was fun," or "Thanks a lot, see you soon." It's impolite to suddenly appear in your coat, saying goodbye without any warning that you were thinking of leaving.

Part of growing up is knowing that when you've spent a

lot of time at a friend's house you should invite him to yours. No better way of inviting him has been found than: "It's your turn to come to my house. . . ."

When you visit an apartment in a big city you'll sometimes find buildings with buzzer systems that you have to operate before the main lobby door will open for you. Here's what you do:

1. Find your friend's family name by looking at the names attached to the mailboxes.

2. Over or near each name you'll see a button. Push the button nearest his name, and you'll hear a buzzer sound which means that the lobby door is being automatically opened for you to go in. Before you go through, though, make sure you remember the complete number of the apartment because the first part will indicate which floor you should head for.

3. Don't be frightened if a weird sounding voice comes over the loudspeaker in some buzzer systems. Believe it or not, it's your friend's voice—or someone's in his family— acknowledging your ring and telling you to come on up.

4. Step into the elevator and press the button corresponding to the floor you want; then get out and locate the exact apartment number.

When visitors come to your house let your parents answer the door if they are home. If, however, you're close by and they ask you to answer it, *walk* to the door, open it, and say "Hello." When the visitors are people you know, say "Please come in," then step back so they can *get* in. Close the door and ask, "May I take your coats?" Then hang them up or put them carefully on a chair or bench. Invite them into the living room and say, "I'll tell my mother (father, sister, aunt, etc.) that you're here." Then tell; don't yell. Find your parents and tell them who has arrived. To finish a perfect job, go back to the living room and keep the guests company until your parents arrive.

Conversation
with Adults

Conversation may be difficult, but it's sometimes necessary while you're waiting for your parents to come on the scene. You should be the one to start the conversation, even though it's tempting to wait in silence for a guest to speak first. Sometimes a simple statement about an interesting thing you did that day ("I just got back from my guitar lesson") or are going to do ("I'm going to a good movie this afternoon") is easier than trying to think of a good question. Usually older people will ask you the first question and get you off the hook. Try not to fidget or yawn at times like this, because it makes matters worse. Look at people during a conversation, and listen when they're talking. As soon as you can, get out of the habit of saying "Huh?" when you don't understand something. Say "What?" or "Excuse me?" or "I beg your pardon."

Sometimes you'll get a long drawn-out story but even then, try to avoid staring at an invisible sympathizer as if to say, "Will this ever end?" Never whisper in front of others —you cut them out as surely as if you'd chased them out of the room and closed the door. When you have something confidential to say to someone, wait until you're alone with him. Whispering always sounds like bad news.

When you receive a compliment, say "Thank you." Accept it as you would a gift—with appreciation, not a shrug of refusal.

Gestures are part of conversation, too. Here are some habits to avoid when you're talking to others:
* Don't stick your hands in your pockets and shift around continuously.
* Don't keep clearing your throat or running your tongue over your teeth or chew gum with sound effects.
* Don't toss an imaginary ball in the air, or practice long passes with a non-existent football, or pretend to take a shot at something.
* Don't scratch your head or crack your knuckles. Sometimes you pick up these disagreeable gestures from your friends without realizing it, so start watching out for them.

When you come home and find your parents entertaining guests, wait a moment in full view of your father or mother to see whether they want you to come into the room. It usually depends on what they are discussing. When you're invited to "come in and say hello," do just that: Say "Hello" to everyone either individually or by saying, "Hello, everybody." If you're not invited to join your parents because of a card game or a serious discussion, go quietly to another part of the house. If it's direly necessary to get your parents' attention, go and stand by one of them and ask to speak to him a moment. You'll rarely get a special favor by interrupting and announcing your desires like a drill sergeant.

When family friends come to the door and your parents aren't home, ask them to come in and only then say, "Mother and Dad aren't home right now." Let them decide whether they'd like to stay awhile and visit with you, or go. Don't open the door and announce that your parents aren't home while the callers are standing outside—it's too much like asking, "Friend or foe?"

On the Telephone

Telephones are not walkie-talkies for barking orders and emergency messages. When you place or receive a telephone call, it's almost like greeting a guest at the door. Because you can't see people's faces by telephone (at present, that is, but science promises to remedy this drawback very soon), your voice and what you say are very important.

When you answer the phone—Say "Hello" in a pleasant voice. Don't say "Yes?" impatiently, or—like a junior butler—"Jimmy Jones' residence!"

If the call is for you, say "This is Jimmy speaking"; not "This is me."

If the call is for someone else in the family, say "Just a moment, please, and I'll call him." Then don't give out with an ear-splitting scream, but go find the other person and tell him he's wanted on the phone.

When you are called to the phone, start by saying "Hello," instead of "Who is it?"

When the call is for someone who isn't home, say "My mother isn't at home; may I take a message?" Never hesitate to ask for the spelling of someone's name. Say, "Will you please spell your name for me?" if you're not sure of it.

When the doorbell rings while you're talking on the phone, say "Excuse me," answer the door and—if they are friends —invite them in, then return to the phone and tell your caller you'll have to call him back later.

The person who places a call should be the first to say good-bye. If you find this difficult at times, try saying "I have to finish my homework now" or "I have to go now; someone else wants to use the phone." You should limit the length of your telephone calls to five or six minutes; and call your friends at reasonable times: never before breakfast or after 9 P.M. unless it's an emergency.

Some Kind Thoughts

When you are around handicapped people, the hardest but most important thing is to treat them like everyone else. Don't change the way you normally talk or act. In other words, be yourself as much as you can. Also, keep these facts in mind:

Blind people are not deaf, so you don't have to talk louder. When you're talking to a blind person use his name as often as possible, because that is his only way of knowing you're addressing *him*. When you first meet a blind person, even if he knows you well, identify yourself: Say, "Hi, I'm Jim Jones" or "Hello, Mrs. Smith—Margy Brown." And always tell a blind person what you're offering him: "Here's your sandwich, Bill" or "This is the iced tea you wanted, Mrs. Johnson."

Deaf people prefer to read lips or to follow their own methods of hearing you; so don't raise your voice around them. Always keep your head turned toward a deaf person when you are speaking, although you don't have to keep your eyes focused on him. Never point out to a newcomer that someone is deaf—it doesn't help anyone or anything.

Say good morning—or at least "Hi" to each member of your family when you first see him in the morning.

Answer when you're spoken to—Say, "Yes, mother"; "No, mother"; "Yes, dad"; "No, dad" instead of Yah, Unhuh, Nope, and Naw, which are noises, not words.

Say hello to your father when he comes home from work—Just a simple, "Hi, dad" as he takes off his coat reminds him of what he's working for—you, mostly.

Let your family know when you come and go—You're home and all's well. You're off to a pal's for a while. You're going to buy some bicycle tape. It's important to let your parents know—they relax when they're sure of what you're up to. The more cooperative you are about your plans, the more cooperative they'll be.

Return or replace what you borrow—and believe it or not, others will do the same for you!

Say "Sorry" when you bump into someone, step on a toe, or get in someone's way—and that goes for young and old, male and female victims.

Stand up when your mother comes into a room and offer her a chair if she's going to sit down. Hold her chair for her when she comes to the dining room table. Then you'll remember to do this for other women.

Open doors for your mother and sisters—for all women, as a matter of fact, and let them go ahead of you.

Carry packages for your mother or any woman you're walking with. This includes sisters.

Say "Thank you" and "Please" when you ask for something or get it. These may have been your first words of good manners, but no matter how tall in the saddle you get, they're still your most powerful weapons.

Pay your debts, even if it's only a dime you owe your little sister. It's the only way to avoid becoming a dead beat, a beggar, or a bad risk. If you're broke, offer to do an errand or a chore; then pay what you owe on the spot.

Observe others' privacy—and you'll get the privacy *you* want for your own room, possessions, mail, books, or collections.

When you share a room, do your share of housekeeping—particularly in the bathroom. Hang up towels, put your own stuff where it belongs, and clean the bathtub before you leave.

Say goodnight to your parents when you're ready to go to bed. You don't believe in ghosts any more, so why disappear like one yourself?

Flying the
American Flag

The flag may be flown any day from sunrise to sunset, but it should not be raised if it's raining, and it should be lowered as soon as rain starts. When a flag is worn or damaged, it should not be displayed, but should be privately burned.

FLY YOUR FLAG ON THESE SPECIAL DAYS:

Inauguration Day—January 20
Lincoln's Birthday—February 12
Washington's Birthday—February 22
Memorial Day—May 30 (Flag is half-staffed until noon, then full-staffed until sunset)
Flag Day—June 14
Independence Day—July 4
Labor Day—First Monday in September
Constitution Day—September 17
Columbus Day—October 12
Veterans' Day—November 11

DISPLAY YOUR FLAG LIKE THIS:

From your house on a hanger from the front of your house, or on a flag pole, with the Union part of the flag all the way to the top of the staff.

On a wall or in a window—Flattened out, never draped, with the Union section in the upper left hand corner.

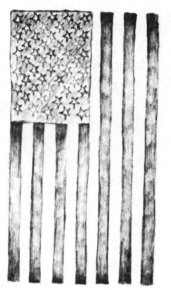

Conducting a Meeting

Life is made up of meetings. If you haven't already, you'll probably soon be busy with a club of your own and going to Scout or school meetings. Later on in high school there'll be Student Council meetings; in college, fraternity meetings; and—after you're married—PTA meetings, business meetings, right through to Chairman-of-the-Board meetings. So every boy should know how to conduct a meeting properly, because even billion-dollar mergers are based on the same rules you'll use to decide how the club house should be built and who'll be allowed to use it. These rules are called Parliamentary Rules because they were originally set up by the Parliament of England and were so good they were copied throughout the world. The word Parliament comes from the French word *parler*, to speak, and that is the reason for rules in the first place: to give everyone a chance to speak his mind, but in an orderly and fair way.

Anyone who can conduct a meeting is about ten steps ahead of everyone else, because he's looked up to and respected as a leader.

Before you hold a meeting, you need club officers: a president, a vice president to take the place of the president when he's sick or out of town, a secretary to take notes of everything that goes on during each meeting, and a treasurer to collect money or dues, to keep a record of it, and to guard it with his life. You also need members, of course, because meetings should be held only when there is a majority of members present. Majority means half the membership plus one more person. You don't need a constitution, but you should be clear about what your club hopes to do or stand for.

And above all you need a good gavel, which is a wooden hammer. If you don't have one, use any hard object to pound on the table; that is how you get order and keep everyone from speaking at once.

HERE IS THE WAY A MEETING IS CONDUCTED:

The person who conducts the meeting is called a chairman. He is usually the president of the club, but if you have no elected officers, you appoint someone to conduct the meeting and he automatically becomes the chairman.

The chairman calls the meeting to order—He taps the table with the gavel and says, "The meeting is called to order."

The secretary reads the minutes of the last meeting—Minutes are a short but accurate written report of what goes on during every meeting. They are not actually a minute-by-minute repeat of every word spoken, every insult, every crazy idea—that would be too long and boring—but an outline of what has been talked about (in the same order it was discussed) and how the voting went.

The chairman asks the members to approve the minutes—He says, "If there are no objections, the minutes are approved" or ". . . the minutes stand as read." Sometimes a member will have an objection or correction. In that case, he raises his hand for permission to speak and then states his correction. The chairman must then ask the group to vote to add the correction to the minutes. He says, "All in favor of adding Herb's correction to the minutes say 'Aye.' "

The chairman then calls on special committees to give reports—He can say, "Will the Finance Committee please report on the amount of money we raised last week on the book sale?" or "Will the Food Committee please tell us what each person has to bring for next Saturday's overnight hike?"

Old or unfinished business left over from the last meeting is taken up next—Suppose everyone had to go home last week before the club settled several problems. The chairman says, "We will now take up unfinished business." Then any member of the club can raise his hand for permission to speak. The Chairman recognizes him, which means he nods and says, "Yes, Maurie?" Then Maurie stands up and suggests what he thinks the club should discuss first in unfinished business. In order that no one member can harp on some old favorite subject too often, the chairman asks, "Will someone second Maurie's motion that we discuss the naming of our mascot?" Until someone seconds the motion (He says, "I second the motion"), the motion can't be discussed.

After old business, the chairman opens the meeting to new business—Usually it is up to the chairman to carry the ball on new business. He should lead the group and take the responsibility of suggesting what he thinks is important or urgent to decide. He then says, "The meeting is now open for motions of new business." As soon as a member has the floor to speak, he says, "I make a motion to change this club's insignia, because everyone in the neighborhood is copying us." Or, "I make a motion to buy a new lock for the club room door because the girls have learned the old combination." Someone has to second the motion before the rest of the members can get to their feet and give their opinions. When all discussion is over and no one else is asking to speak, the chairman has to sense that the subject is exhausted and say, "We will now vote on the motion that. . . ."

The club votes—First the secretary reads aloud exactly what is being voted on so that everybody understands. Then the chairman asks for a voice vote. If there's any doubt, he asks for a show of hands or a roll call vote. In a roll call vote, each member stands up when his name is called and says how he votes.

The meeting is ended by adjourning it—The chairman says, "I move to adjourn this meeting; will those in favor say aye?" Everybody's hungry by then, anyway, so the ayes usually win.

Note: These are the bare bones on holding a meeting, but if you'd really like to get into the fine points of the subject get *Robert's Rules of Order,* a book that almost every meeting in America follows.

Dances and Dancing School

Do you know that in China they still have an ancient dance called "The Battle-Ax"? Tribes used to dance it to show they were ready to strike, to go into battle if necessary. And perhaps, who knows, there is also a dance called "The Trembling Leaf"—for a tribe too scared to move. Dancing is that old. It goes back 50,000 years when only men and boys danced. Girls weren't allowed to learn until just a few hundred years ago, and although they have caught on very fast, they are just as self-conscious and scared at their first dance as boys are. They huddle in groups, whispering and giggling, while boys try not to do a "Battle-Ax" or a "Trembling Leaf."

Boys rarely go to dances until sixth grade or junior high school, but you should learn how to dance and how to behave on a dance floor as near the fifth grade as possible. If you're fortunate, you'll start attending a dancing school around the age of ten. It may seem boring and a waste of time, but everything you learn in dancing class—even the basic steps which teach rhythm and body coördination—are as valuable later on as swimming lessons would be to a fellow who suddenly falls off a boat. It may be true that "if you can walk, you can dance," but you probably fell down a lot before you walked perfectly, so you're bound to need a lot of practice before you dance well. In addition to all kinds of dances, you'll learn special manners that will get you out of many sticky situations when you go away to boarding school, college, or to your first job.

If dancing classes are out of the question, you can still learn to dance at home; your parents or an older brother or sister can teach you, and you can pick up valuable help by watching teen dances on television. Unfortunately, however, your family can't go along with you to the dance itself, so here is what you can expect when you're invited to a dance or a dancing school:

1. Clothes—These days there is so much variation in clothes that it's wise to find out what should be worn before you go. In most dancing schools, boys wear blazers or sport jackets, ties, and white or pale colored shirts. They polish their shoes, leave their bubble gum at home, and in other words try to look great. However, at many school dances, jeans, turtlenecks, and sneakers are the old reliables and anyone dressed-up would look as if he were going to church!

2. When you arrive at the dance or the dancing class, you take off your outer coat and hang it wherever things are being kept. Usually boys' coats are in one place, girls' in another.

3. You greet your hostess or teacher before greeting anyone else you know, but you always remove your topcoat before greeting a hostess.

4. You tell her your name because no one can remember everyone's name in a group. The moment you say "Good evening, Mrs. Smith; I'm Jeremy Jones," you take her off the hook in case she doesn't recognize you with hair combed and that new blazer on. If there is more than one hostess or chaperon standing there, you do the same thing

right down the receiving line. You never say, "I'm Mister (or Master) Jones"; in fact, men never call *themselves* Mister, they simply say their full names.

5. You shake hands with a hostess when you say hello to her.

6. When you go into the dance or onto the dance floor, you'll probably find girls on one side of the room, boys on the other. Go where the boys are and hopefully you'll find someone you know to talk to and stand with until the music and dancing begin.

7. Until you're much older, dancing will be directed by a teacher or a chaperon. Sometimes the dance will be "Boys ask girls," sometimes "Girls ask boys," sometimes "Stags (extra boys) choose first." Go along with it, and very soon you'll decide which girls you really like dancing with.

8. When they announce a "Boys ask girls" dance, go get a partner. Don't stand back and nod your head or curve your finger at a girl; go over and ask her to dance. You can say, "Shall we?" or "May I have this dance?" or you can just smile and say hello. The important thing is to approach the girl and not make her come over to you.

9. Cutting in is usually allowed and encouraged at dances (up until older, high school groups, where it's frowned upon because of dating). To cut in, you simply tap the boy's shoulder and he releases the girl to dance with you. You don't have to say anything, and the girl never refuses, nor does the boy she's dancing with. At private dances, and many dancing classes, extra boys are invited for the express purpose of cutting in; it adds excitement and keeps the scene changing. A girl feels twice as pretty when somone cuts in!

10. At the end of a number, you thank the girl you've

been dancing with. You can say, "That was great" or "Thanks" or "Swell"; anything. Then take her back to her group, or sit down with her. You never walk away and leave her stranded on the dance floor, nor do you find her a chair and then leave with a sigh of relief. After all, she's not a package you had to deliver, and you're not an errand boy!

11. When you sit with a girl, you allow her to sit on *your right*. If another girl or a woman comes over to talk to you or to sit with you, stand up and remain standing until she sits down or leaves.

12. Refreshments are usually served at a certain time which will be announced; they're almost always punch and cookies or "those same old macaroons." You serve the girl by going over and getting two cups of punch, two napkins, and some cookies. Then you take them back to where the girl is sitting, or hand hers to her if she has come along with you to the refreshment table.

Never leave cookies on a chair seat when you're finished, and always return empty cups and glasses to the table.

13. Later on, at teen-age and high school dances, there may be a continuous buffet of soft drinks, sandwiches, candy, etc., so that whenever you feel like it you can say, "Let's get something to eat" and wander over to the table with your partner—but you still serve the girl first!

14. Avoid rough-housing and hacking around at dances, even if you're not having a whale of a time. Don't mishandle or break furniture or get into tussles with other boys. Save your steam for the walk home.

15. Boys rarely give girls corsages these days. Giving a girl a corsage is as OUT as bowing to her when you ask her to dance. However, in certain areas and cities, when boys are old enough to wear dinner jackets and girls are old

enough to wear a long or short formal dress, the boy does send the girl a corsage of small flowers or a single gardenia or camellia. And she is duty-bound to wear it on her dress or at her wrist unless she wants to break his heart. Most corsages end up beautifying and perfuming the top rack of the refrigerator as long as the memory of the dance lingers on.

16.   When the dance is over, you say goodnight to your hostess, shake hands, and if it has been a private party, you thank her. Then, and only then, you get your coat and put it on. Never say goodnight after you've put on your coat, and never try to save time by smuggling out your coat in one hand while shaking hands with the other. Try to get your *own* coat when you leave; it's difficult to make a switch from the other end of town when you wear another boy's coat home by mistake.

Note: When you're older and away at school or college, you will write a note to thank your hostess for inviting you to a private dance or any party in her house.

Part-Time Jobs

Somehow boys who work seem to grow up faster and more easily. Having a job builds muscles, a feeling of manliness, *and* a savings account. So although you have to be sixteen years old in most states before an employer can hire you full-time, there's no reason why you can't work part-time after school and during summer vacation.

Did you know that you can get a Social Security card from the first day you're born, and that you can open a savings account at any age? Therefore, as soon as you're able to follow through on a job, here are a few you can consider:

Lawn and sidewalk care—Raking leaves, cleaning up lawns, sweeping sidewalks, pulling weeds (be sure you know a weed when you see one; and if you're in doubt, ask the person you're working for—*he'll* know!), mowing grass with a manual mower or even with a power mower if you're over twelve and know how to handle one.

Apple (or any other fruit) picking—From the trees when fruit is ripe and from the ground when rotting fruit begins to fall.

Snow shoveling by the job or by the hour—Ask around before you set your price, or better still, make a deal before you start each job; then there won't be any misunderstanding. We know one nine-year-old who always shovels free the first time, then knocks on the door, announces his gen-

110

erosity and says that from now on he will do the job for X number of dollars each time. It works.

Paper routes—The single most popular and dependable way to make money without going too far from home. But there's plenty of competition for good routes, so you have to be reliable. Work up from a small route of about twenty houses to as many as you can handle without getting all tired out.

Errand boy—Put your name, address, working hours, and telephone number on a few plain index cards and then hand them out around your neighborhood. State the round-trip price—usually 25¢—for such errands as delivering or picking up packages from local stores, etc.

Delivery boy—For local grocery stores, florists, drugstores, hardware stores, any small businesses.

Supermarket jobs—In some areas you can get a job bagging groceries on Saturdays even if you're not sixteen years old. It depends on your own city and state laws.

Baby sitting—From twelve years on, you can usually get a few jobs baby sitting, especially when it's more sitting than babying, and particularly when the jobs are in nearby houses so you can call on your mother or older sister for assistance. Otherwise, most mothers insist that baby sitters be at least fourteen years old.

Outdoor nursery—Start a neighborhood service to look after and play with toddlers in a safe area of your own yard while their mothers go to the hairdresser or do their shopping. This is a good idea for weekends and summer days, and you can specify the hours you'll be available: 10:00 A.M. to 12 noon; 2:00 to 4:00 P.M., for instance.

Car washing—Any Saturday morning you and the gang can go around the neighborhood and offer to wash a car or two for whatever the traffic will bear, usually $1.00 or $1.50 maximum, using your own supplies. If you're lucky enough to have a big garage area at home, you can make a sign and alert the neighbors to your Car Wash, but have your pail, soap, hoses, and polishing cloths all set to speed up the job.

Store helper—Not to handle money or sales, but to dust and straighten shelves and merchandise, sweep floors, clean stockrooms, answer the phone, or run errands.

HOW TO GET THE JOB

The best way is to apply in person, because an employer can judge you by your appearance (neat and clean), your manner (polite, wide-awake, good clear voice), your age (it's better not to lie because sooner or later he will ask to see your Social Security card, etc.), and also he can ask you important questions.

The best "opening" is the simple fact that you are looking for a part-time job; so say it, but with enthusiasm and interest.

Another way is to telephone. Ask to speak to the owner, manager, or proprietor of the store and then tell him your name, your age, and your request: "I'm Joey Brown, I'm thirteen years old, and I'm looking for a part-time job. Do you have an opening for an errand or delivery boy in your store?" It's often a good idea to tell him you live nearby and give your address, so he will know he's hiring a member of his own community.

A third way is sometimes necessary: writing for a job.

This could be the case when you are applying for a paper route. Remember that your letter has to make a good impression *for* you, so take time with spelling, good handwriting, and neatness. Address the envelope and the letter itself to the Circulation Manager, Name of Newspaper, Street address, City and Zone number. In the letter write: "Dear Mr. Jones, I am looking for a paper route in my neighborhood, and would like you to consider me for one of the Name-of-Newspaper routes. I am _____ years old, attend _____ school in the _____ grade, and I think I can do a good job for you. If there is a route available, I would appreciate a call from you. My telephone number is _____ _____. Yours truly," and sign your full name with pen and ink even if you have typed the main body of the letter. Be sure your address is in the upper right-hand corner of the letter under the date.

TO KEEP THE JOB

Reliability is the main thing. Be on time, be dependable, and don't ask for too many days or hours off, even if it's for school work. Be honest, accurate, and cheerful—or at least interested in your work. No one likes to see a slave-in-chains look on an employee's face when he reports in. And no employer likes to keep reminding you of the essentials in your work. For instance, if you have a paper route and your Circulation Manager insists on papers being placed on doorsteps, he'll blow his top if you continue to toss them behind shrubbery and through windows.

THE PLUS FACTORS OF PART-TIME JOBS

You accumulate references for full-time jobs later on. If you ever want to be a newspaper copy boy in the Editorial office, one of the world's best references is that you delivered the paper from the time you were eleven years old.

You can save money for important things: a racing bike, a college education, a car, special sports equipment. And do you know about *interest?* That's the money a bank *pays you* for using your money; it really adds up once you've started depositing money on which interest can be computed. If you've never been able to get to a bank because of school hours, find out how to bank by mail—it's the new thing to do, and it guarantees you at least one letter a week when the bank mails back your deposit slip.

Reference File of Now and Future Things to Know

A

Addressing an envelope—Start in the middle of the envelope, to leave space for the stamp and the return address. Using ink, not pencil, write the person's or company's full name on the first line. Then indent about one-half inch and write the street address on the second line. Indent again, and on the third line write the City (comma) State (spelled out, not abbreviated) and zone number. The envelope should match your writing paper. Address boys under sixteen as Master Tom Jones, not Mr. Tom Jones.

B

Buttons—In an emergency you should know how to sew on a button. First, remember boys' buttons are always on the right side of a shirt, jacket, or coat. (Women's buttons are sewed on the left side. Once all buttons were on the left side, but during the Middle Ages men's were changed to the right, so a man could quickly unbutton his coat with his left hand while reaching for his sword with his right hand.)

116

To sew on a button with holes in it, thread a needle and knot the two ends together to make a double strand. Take one stitch on top of the fabric exactly where you want the button to go; the button will hide the knot. Push the needle up through the first hole and down through the next, straight through the fabric itself. Sew up and down through fabric and button holes about five times, then knot the thread on the under side of the fabric.

For a stronger job on a suit or coat button, tailors say to put a straight pin across the top of the button and sew over it four or five times as you go up and down through fabric and button holes. Then remove the pin and wrap the thread around and around to form a "stem" under the button. Knot it on the under side of the fabric.

Boats—Have decks, and all decks are ruined by leather soles and heels; so wear sneakers or go barefoot.

Are limited in space. Take aboard a minimum of clothing and keep track of it.

Have special terms: Stairs are *ladders;* walls are *bulkheads;* the front of the boat is the *bow;* the rear is the *stern;* the kitchen is the *galley;* the bed is a *bunk;* and the toilet is the *head. Starboard* is the right-hand side when you're facing forward; *portside* is the left-hand side.

Can be dangerous: Keep out of the way, duck the boom on a sailboat, sit down when you're told and where you're told to, especially before a speedboat takes off or you'll be tossed backward into the propeller.

Have one basic law: You have to obey the captain. He's responsible for your safety and the ship's.

Have a leeward and windward side—If you have to toss something overboard, toss it to the sheltered (leeward) side. It's better to wait and dispose of trash on shore.

C

Camp letters—When you're away at camp, write to your grandmother, grandfather, aunts, or uncles in addition to the one letter home required by the camp each week. In return, you may get cookies, candy bars, even money—but you'll certainly get a few letters just when you begin to feel homesick.

Creeps, losers—Don't be too quick to label a new boy a creep or a loser just because he's different or a newcomer in school or the neighborhood. Hold it; he may be your best friend next week!

COLORS AND HOW THEY GO TOGETHER

What Goes With What

SUIT	SHIRT	TIE	SOCKS	SHOES
BLUE	White	Gray	Blue	Black
	Blue	Blue	Black	Dark Brown
	Gray	Wine	Black	Black
GRAY	White	Blue	Blue	Black
	Gray	Black	Black	Black
	Gray	Green	Green	Black
	Blue	Wine	Wine	Brown
	Ivory	Gold	Wine	Brown
BROWN	White	Wine	Wine	Brown
	Tan	Blue	Blue	Brown
	Tan	Green	Green	Brown
	Light Blue	Wine	Wine	Brown
	Ivory	Gold	Brown	Brown
	Ivory	Brown	Brown	Brown
OLIVE	White	Olive	Olive	Brown
	Blue (light)	Blue	Black	Black
	Ivory	Gold	Brown	Brown
	Olive	Brown	Brown	Brown
	Tan	Wine	Brown	Brown

D

Dating—Doesn't belong in your life until you're in high school.

Doctors, dentists—When you have an appointment at the dentist's or doctor's, be on time or a bit early, take your own book to read in case there's a wait, wear clean and neat clothes, and try to brush your teeth before a visit to the dentist. Things will go more smoothly if you don't act as if you're entering a torture chamber.

E

Exercises can be your secret muscle-building weapon if you do them every morning before you go to school. The three best ones are push-ups, sit-ups (with arms outstretched or bent behind your head), and jumping rope (ask any prize fighter!).

F

First names—You shouldn't call older people by their first names until you're requested to—by them.

G

Gent or *gents*—Words to forget. Say *gentleman* and *gentlemen*.

Golf has special rules:

Wear rubber-soled or spiked shoes, never leather-soled ones—they're slippery and they leave deep marks on the greens.

Walk on greens as little as possible to avoid leaving indentations.

Each player keeps track of his own score which he announces at the end of each hole, not stroke by stroke. Then whoever is holding the score card marks it up.

The ball farthest from the hole is shot first.

When you lose a ball, signal players behind you to go through while you hunt for it; then wait for that group to play past you before continuing.

When your opponent loses a ball, help him find it, but give up if you don't locate it quickly or you'll hold up the group behind you.

You can't claim "a ball out of the blue" until it stops rolling so don't run to grab one from an unseen player.

When you're a spectator at a match, don't move, talk, or stand close when the player is making a stroke. Remember those matches on TV—so quiet you think the sound has gone off!

H

Home—A place to make the people around you glad you're there and sorry to see you go out.

I

Invite—is never used in place of the word invitation. You don't give or receive an invite to a party; you receive an invitation.

Ironing a shirt—Can be a terrifying task if you don't know these few hints for a good result in that moment of crisis:

1. The collar is the most important thing, especially the points; so start by ironing the *underside* of the points, pushing the iron up from the points toward the middle of the collar.

2. Next, iron the yoke of the shirt around the shoulders.

3. Then iron the collar itself; underside first, top side last.

4. Then the cuffs, inside and out.

5. The body of the shirt can be ironed last.

J

Jokes can make you popular, except when they're cruel: Jokes about girls who wear glasses, girls who still have their baby fat, or who aren't as pretty as your dream girl.

K

Kissing and being kissed by relatives or your parents' friends are one of the embarrassments in a boy's life, but don't try to duck or run away—they'll catch you anyway. and then it's a real production. Bear up, get it over with, and someday you'll find out about the pleasant aspects of kissing.

L

Leave me—Means "depart from me," but if that isn't what you mean, say *"Let* me do it," or *"Let* me have a turn."

122

Letters to important people
How to address the President, the Vice President, U. S.
and State Senators and Congressmen, the mayor, governor,
and the clergy.

The President of the U.S.

Address:	The President
	The White House
	Washington, D.C.
Letter Opening:	Dear Mr. President:
	or
	Mr. President:
Closing:	Respectfully,
Speak of him as:	The President
Call him:	Mr. President or Sir
Introduce him as:	"Mr. President, may I present . . .
Say:	"How do you do, Mr. President."

The President's Wife

Address:	Mrs. Neilson
	The White House
	Washington, D.C.
Letter Opening:	Dear Mrs. Neilson:
Closing:	Sincerely,
Speak of her as:	Mrs. Neilson
Call her:	Mrs. Neilson
Introduce her as:	"Mrs. Neilson, may I present . . ."
Say:	"How do you do, Mrs. Neilson."
Envelope address	
for both:	The President and Mrs. Neilson.

United States
and
State Senators

Address: The Honorable James A. Lee
                             United States Senate
                             Washington, D.C.
                             or
                             The Honorable John J. Day
                             State Capitol
                             Springfield, Illinois

Letter Opening: Dear Senator Lee:
Closing: Respectfully,
Speak of him as: The Senator or Senator Lee
Call him: Senator Lee
Introduce him as: "Senator Lee, may I present . . ."
Say: "How do you do, Senator Lee,"
                             or "How do you do, Senator."

To address Senator   The Honorable James A. Lee
Lee and his wife: and Mrs. Lee.

Members of Congress
or
State Legislature

Address: The Honorable Charles A.
                             Lindsay
                             United States House of
                             Representatives
                             Washington, D.C.
                             or
                             The Honorable John A. Dix
                             State Capitol
                             Des Moines, Iowa

124

Letter Opening:	Dear Mr. Lindsay:
Closing:	Respectfully,
Speak of him as:	Mr. Lindsay
Call him:	Mr. Lindsay
Introduce him as:	"Mr. Lindsay, may I present . . ."
Say:	"How do you do, Mr. Lindsay."
To address Mr. Lindsay and his wife:	The Honorable Charles A. Lindsay and Mrs. Lindsay

A Governor

Address:	The Honorable Samuel E. Walsh Governor of California The Governor's Mansion Sacramento, California
Letter Opening:	Dear Governor Walsh:
Closing:	Respectfully,
Speak of him as:	The Governor
Call him:	Governor Walsh or Sir
Introduce him as:	"Governor Walsh, may I present . . ."
Say:	"How do you do, Governor Walsh."
To address the Governor and his wife:	"The Honorable Samuel Walsh and Mrs. Walsh."

The Mayor

Address:	The Honorable Emerit Lindbeck Mayor of Kewanee City Hall Kewanee, Illinois
Letter Opening:	Dear Mayor Lindbeck:
Closing:	Respectfully,

Speak of him as:	The Mayor or Mayor Lindbeck
Call him:	Mayor Lindbeck or Sir
Introduce him as:	"Mayor Lindbeck, may I present . . ."
Say:	"How do you do, Mr. Mayor," or "How do you do, Mayor Lindbeck."
To address the Mayor and his wife:	The Honorable Emerit Lindbeck and Mrs. Lindbeck.

A Minister

Address:	The Reverend Samuel Simpson (plus any title) or The Reverend Dr. Samuel Simpson
Letter Opening:	Dear Mr. Simpson: or Dear Dr. Simpson:
Closing:	Sincerely,
Speak of him as:	Mr. (or Dr.) Simpson
Call him:	Mr. (or Dr.) Simpson
Introduce him as:	"Dr. Simpson, may I present . . ."
To address a clergyman and his wife:	The Reverend Samuel Simpson and Mrs. Simpson or The Right Reverend Samuel Simpson and Mrs. Simpson

A Priest

Address:	The Reverend Daniel W. Williams (or other initials indicating his order, if he belongs to one) Pastor, St. Peter's Church, City and State

Letter Opening:	Dear Father Williams:
Closing:	Sincerely,
Speak of him as:	Father Williams
Call him:	Father Williams
Introduce him as:	"Father Williams, may I present . . ."
Say:	"How do you do, Father Williams," or "How do you do, Father."

A Rabbi

Address:	Rabbi David Rosenberg
Letter Opening:	Dear Rabbi Rosenberg:
Closing:	Sincerely,
Speak of him as:	Rabbi Rosenberg
Call him:	Rabbi Rosenberg
Introduce him as:	"Rabbi Rosenberg, may I present . . ."
Say:	"How do you do, Rabbi Rosenberg," or just "How do you do, Rabbi."

M

Menu translations—Someday when you eat out and want to do the ordering by yourself, you can cram on these English meanings for foods on menus written in French or Italian:

Main Courses (*Entrées*)

Agneau or mouton—Lamb or mutton
Boeuf—Beef

Jambon—Ham
Porc—Pork (you guessed it!)
Foie—Liver
Langue—Tongue
Saucisse, saucisson—Sausage
Bifteck—Steak
Côtes—Chops
Canard—Duck
Poulet—Chicken

Vegetables and Side Dishes

Oeufs—Eggs
Pommes de Terre—Potatoes
Nouilles—Noodles
Pasta—Any spaghetti or noodle dish
Riz—Rice
Riso—Also rice
Artichauts—Artichokes
Asperges—Asparagus
Champignons—Mushrooms
Haricots Verts—Green beans
Petits Pois—Peas
Chou—Cabbage
Laitue—Lettuce
Salade Verte—Salad
Concombre—Cucumber

Sauces

Au Gratin—Cheese sauce
Au Jus—Juice of the meat or meat gravy
Hollandaise—Butter and egg yolk sauce
Tartar Sauce—A fish sauce of mayonnaise, pickles, herbs

Desserts
   Gâteau—Cake
   Tarte—Pie or tart
   Glace—Ice cream
   Flan—Custard
   Pâtisserie—Pastry
   Mousse—Fluffy cream pudding, often chocolate

N

New boy in school—When you have to change schools, don't try to be popular right off the bat. You'll get lots of attention anyway, because you'll be a curiosity that first day.
Don't brag about how far ahead your old school was, and don't boast about your father's job or salary, your family's house, car, etc. Play it cool and quiet.

O

Obscenities are any four-letter words you've picked up lately, and they all belong out of the house and away from mixed company or girls.

Off me, off him—Unless you really peeled it off, you "got this book *from* him," and "he borrowed a quarter *from* you."

P

Pledge of Allegiance—Learn it:

   "I pledge allegiance to the flag of the United States of America and to the Republic for which it stands; one nation, under God, indivisible, with liberty and justice for all."

Q

Quitters—Spoil the fun for others and give themselves a bad name that often covers up their really fine qualities. So don't quit when you're playing badly, and never when you're losing.

R

Return addresses—belong on all envelopes you mail, especially these days when the U.S. Post Office has such a burden: Last year, it delivered 79,500,000,000 (that's almost 80 *billion*) pieces of mail!

S

Swimming Rules

Never swim alone, no matter how good you are: anyone can get a cramp.

Don't dive until you know the depth of the water. Swim in first and find out how deep it is.

Take a shower before you swim in public pools. They all provide showers.

Don't run or wrestle around the edge of a pool unless you want to spend the rest of the summer lounging around in your cast.

Skiing Tips

Wear lightweight clothing because skiing is hot exercise even in below-zero temperatures. Wear clothes that keep you dry.

Goggles or good sunglasses are a necessity; also a cap that won't blow off.

Ski with straps or laces that fasten your skis to your boot binding. Then if you fall your ski won't zoom away from you and hurt other skiers.

Ski at your own pace, and when you fall, fill in the hole with snow before going on.

Let the least skilled skier set the speed for the group; then you won't lose him.

Stay with an injured skier, keep him warm, send someone else for help, and don't move him if you think a bone is broken.

T

Tennis

When you play, wear white if you possibly can: white shorts, shirt, socks, and sneakers. Colors make it difficult to see the ball.

Never go on a court with anything but sneakers—they're the only shoes that protect the court and your own footing.

The server is the one who keeps score and announces it.

To return balls to the server, wait until the point has been made, then collect all balls on your side and return them one by one in a series.

Players change courts after the first, third, fifth, etc. (odd number) games so that neither side or player has the sun in his eyes all the time.

When you're a spectator during the game, don't applaud, shout, or comment on every score. Applaud only good points, not errors, even if they help your side.

Don't move from one match to another until play is over.

Tipping

Taxi Drivers

When fare is between 50¢ and $1.00 .... 25¢
When fare is between $1.00 and $2.00 .... 35¢
When fare is over $2.00 ...... 15 percent of the fare

In Restaurants

The Maître d'hôtel—When he just shows you to your table—No tip.

The Captain—Because he takes drink orders and explains certain parts of the menu for you—5 percent of the bill; never less than $1.00.

Waiter, Waitress—In ordinary restaurant—15 percent of the bill. In luxury restaurants or night clubs—20 percent of the bill.

The Busboy—No tip.

Checkroom Attendant—For a coat, hat, or package—25¢.

Soda Fountain—For drinks or ice cream only—No tip.

Lunch Counter—When any food is ordered—15 percent of the bill; never less than 10¢.

Club Service or Drive-In—When food is ordered—15

percent of the bill unless there's a sign saying "No Tipping."

U

Unpack your clothes and things when you are a house guest for more than one night. Don't rummage through your suitcase ten times a day until it looks like a tossed salad.

V

Visits with your parents to their friends—Say hello, shake hands, stick around for a few minutes, but then don't just sit there and un-enjoy yourself. Ask if there's a TV set you can watch, go for a walk, or find a place to read. Maybe while you're sitting there, someone your own age will wander in.

W

Worst offense in table manners across the country is the improper and awkward handling of knife and fork in cutting meat. The fork should not be held straight up like a dagger. Both knife and fork handles should be in the palm of the hands while cutting.

X

X-rays don't hurt a bit; they're as painless as a photograph of what's on the *outside* of you. And they're speedy, especially if you hold still. All you have to do is uncover the part where the bone might be broken.

Y

Younger people are always introduced to older people. The older person is more important; so say his or her name first: "Mrs. Swanson, this is my sister Jenny."

Z

Zig-zag means the style of eating where you transfer the fork back to your right hand after you've used it in your left hand to cut meat. It's also called the "American style" because that's the way most people use their knives and forks in this country. It's explained on page 60.

This Is Not the End...

This is the end of the book, but it is not the end of good manners—it's just the beginning. You can't be expected to remember everything we told you in one reading, so use this book as a constant reference. Browse through it occasionally. When a situation comes up during the day that you aren't sure of, we hope you'll find the answer to your problem here.

Now we're going to tell you a secret, and you should remember it well. Everyone makes mistakes when it comes to manners, and you're going to be surprised, once you know the right way of doing things, at how many grown-ups do things wrong. That's because they never bothered to learn the simple rules of good behavior.

One more thing before we close: As you grow up you're going to be thrust into social problems that you won't know for sure how to handle. Use common sense. Don't be ashamed to ask someone who *does* know the answer, or admit that you're stumped. Even if you're not certain what to tip the waiter or what to wear to a hayride, it's always easier to ask someone than to make an error.

And if you goof, take heart in the immortal words of General Custer who—when asked during the massacre at Little Big Horn why he led his men into an ambush—shrugged his shoulders and said, "Nobody's perfect."